WESLEYAN FOUNDATIONS FOR EVANGELISM

WESLEYAN FOUNDATIONS FOR EVANGELISM

AL TRUESDALE
Editor

THE FOUNDRY
PUBLISHING®

The Foundry Publishing®
PO Box 419527
Kansas City, MO 64141
thefoundrypublishing.com

ISBN 978-0-8341-3829-2

Printed in the
United States of America

Cover design: Arthur Cherry
Interior design: Kevin Williamson

Library of Congress Cataloging-in-Publication Data

Names: Truesdale, Albert, 1941- editor.

Title: Wesleyan foundations for evangelism / Al Truesdale, editor.

Description: Kansas City, MO : The Foundry Publishing, 2020. | Includes bibliographical references. | Summary: "Wesleyan Foundations for Evangelism mines the expertise of pastors, scholars, and other ministry leaders to offer guides and markers for preparing messengers of God's good news. Written from a Wesleyan perspective, contributors explore such topics as the Great Commission today, what it means to be a messenger of the good news of God's kingdom, and the relationship of Christian practices to evangelism and discipleship"-- Provided by publisher.

Identifiers: LCCN 2020020332 (print) | LCCN 2020020333 (ebook) | ISBN 9780834138292 | ISBN 9780834138308 (ebook)

Subjects: LCSH: Evangelistic work. | Theology, Doctrinal.

Classification: LCC BV3795 .W44 2020 (print) | LCC BV3795 (ebook) | DDC 269.088/287--dc23

LC record available at https://lccn.loc.gov/2020020332

LC ebook record available at https://lccn.loc.gov/2020020333

10 9 8 7 6 5 4 3 2 1

CONTENTS

CONTRIBUTORS

Mark Bane, MDiv
Director of Evangelism and New Church Development
Church of the Nazarene USA/Canada

Christi Bennett, PhD
Campus Pastor, Darby Creek Southwest Church of the Nazarene
Orient, Ohio

Kent Brower, PhD
Senior Research Fellow in Biblical Studies
Nazarene Theological College
Manchester, United Kingdom

David A. Busic, DMin
General Superintendent
Church of the Nazarene

T. Scott Daniels, PhD
Senior Minister, Nampa College Church of the Nazarene
Pastoral Scholar in Residence, Northwest Nazarene University
Nampa, Idaho

Timothy R. Gaines, PhD
Associate Professor of Religion
Trevecca Nazarene University
Nashville, Tennessee

Steven Hoskins, PhD
Associate Professor of Religion
Trevecca Nazarene University
Nashville, Tennessee

Tina Pitamber, DMin
Lead Pastor, Solid Rock Community Church of the Nazarene
Richmond Hill, ON, Canada
Multicultural Congregations Strategic Readiness Team
Church of the Nazarene
Canada Central District

Scott Rainey, DMin
Global Director for Sunday School and Discipleship Ministries International
Church of the Nazarene

Carla Sunberg, PhD
General Superintendent
Church of the Nazarene

Josh Sweeden, PhD
Dean of the Faculty
Associate Professor of Church and Society
Nazarene Theological Seminary
Kansas City, Missouri

Al Truesdale, PhD
Emeritus Professor of Philosophy of Religion and Christian Ethics
Nazarene Theological Seminary
Kansas City, Missouri

Grant Zweigle, DMin
Missionary Training Coordinator for Global Missions
Church of the Nazarene
University Service Coordinator, Office of University Mission and Ministry
Northwest Nazarene University
Nampa, Idaho

INTRODUCTION

Gonzales's sermon text struck me as humorous. The setting was the Turbeville Correctional Institution, Turbeville, South Carolina. The text was Hebrews 2:3: "How shall we escape . . . ?" (KJV). However, there was nothing humorous about his impassioned appeal to his fellow prisoners: "Receive Jesus Christ as your Savior and he will completely transform your life, just as he has mine."

Raised in witchcraft, Gonzales was taught to hate the Bible. Nevertheless, one day he discovered a New Testament, with a red cover, lying in the middle of the street. He began to read. He continued until he had finished it. Soon he attended an evangelistic campaign conducted by a nearby church. On his third visit, he could no longer "escape . . . so great a salvation" (v. 3, KJV). As a broken and penitent sinner, Gonzales surrendered his life to Jesus Christ.

As I listened, the Holy Spirit seemed to remind me of the amazing ways Christ works through his church to bring the lost to himself. "The Church exists by mission just as a fire exists by burning," Emil Brunner said.[1]

But "mission" requires equipping.

Initially, Jesus's disciples were willing but not yet equipped. According to the Gospel of Matthew, before Jesus sent his disciples out to "make disciples of all nations" (Matt. 28:19, NIV), he taught that "proclaiming the good news of the kingdom" entails preparation (9:35, NIV). He detailed the kind of community the church must be to bear faithful witness to the gospel (5:3-16; 6:1-24; 7:12, 21-27). By the time we reach the Great Commission, Jesus has delivered five teachings or discourses.[2] Together, they explain the kingdom of God, what entering and living in it requires and what faithful witness to the gospel entails.

Jesus is equipping his church for life and mission in a highly diverse world. Twice Matthew uses the Greek word *ekklēsia* (ek-klay-see-a, an "assembly" or a "convocation"; 16:18; 18:17), translated "church," to indicate the primary audience of his Gospel.

A Christian doesn't have to master the Gospel of Matthew before telling others that through Jesus Christ, old things can pass away and all things become new (2 Cor. 5:17). Nevertheless, solid foundations are imperative for the church.

Church history is littered with persons and institutions that proceeded to speak before clearly understanding the good news of God's kingdom. The book of 2 Samuel tells of a zealous messenger named Ahimaaz. He ran to King David to report on a battle. However, upon arrival, all he could say was that he had heard a lot of noise (18:19-30).

Churches of all sizes and national contexts have an enduring responsibility to prepare members to fulfill Jesus's Great Commission. This should be done in a manner faithful to the God whose mission Christians serve.

This is certainly true of denominations whose understanding of the Christian faith is directly influenced by John and Charles Wesley, founders of Methodism. These denominations hold distinct convictions about Christian discipleship, evangelism, and the church's mission. They believe those convictions are faithful to the Old and New Testaments. Wesleyan foundations for evangelism are simply distinguishing characteristics, identifying markers, and guides. They are certainly not unique among Christians. When correctly understood, they explain the astonishing *mission* of God to redeem his creation. And they show the joyous *mission* God has assigned to the church.

This book rests upon the conviction that a church that evangelizes in accordance with the New Testament should be one where the fruit and gifts of the Holy Spirit are manifest. "Evangelism," says theologian Bryan Stone, "relies from first to last on the beauty of holiness made real in the church by the operation of the Holy Spirit."[3]

Church historian Alan Kreider makes the sobering observation that numerical growth in the early post–New Testament church resulted primarily because Christians "lived by a habitus [virtues, embodied faith] that attracted others." Facing a pagan Greco-Roman world, they believed "when people's lives are rehabilitated in the way of Jesus, others will want to join them." Church growth "was the product, not of the Christians' persuasive powers, but of their convincing lifestyle."[4]

Foundations for evangelism, not *strategies* or *methods*, frame this book.[5]

It locates the Wesleyan family within the broader Christian faith. Then it examines the Great Commission for today. Next, it explains the good news of the kingdom of God and what it means to become a messenger. Subsequent chapters examine distinctive features of Wesleyan theology as they affect evangelism. Chapter 10 explores the relationship between Christian practices, evangelism, and discipleship. Each chapter provides questions for group discussion and additional resources for expanding the topic.

Evangelism needs congregations where the Holy Spirit is trusted, discipleship is being learned and lived, Christian koinonia and holiness are passions, new Christians are being nurtured, and God's love is being expressed to all.

The purpose of this book is to explain Wesleyan foundations for evangelism and to encourage and equip clergy and laypersons who identify with this doctrinal family. At their best, Wesleyan foundations for evangelism are simply *servant vehicles* for telling everyone the God of all mercy and peace is ready to rescue them "from the power of darkness" and transfer them "into the kingdom of his beloved Son" (Col. 1:13, NRSV).

The contributors believe carefully laid foundations can help prepare Christians for effective witness in all contexts.

1

WESLEYANS AND APOSTOLIC CHRISTIAN FAITH

Steven Hoskins, PhD

Al Truesdale, PhD

As a six-year-old, one of us was trapped between his parents on a tent-meeting bench. During the lengthy sermon, he focused on rearranging sawdust with his bare feet. Another of us, as a baby barely two months old, was bathed in the creek at a holiness camp meeting. These were our introductions to the Church of the Nazarene and the Wesleyan theological tradition.

By God's grace, at age seventeen one of us became a Christian and was called into the ordained Christian ministry. The other was converted during a revival at a Nazarene college, followed by a path to ordination. Thus began our journey in Christian discipleship, theological education, and service in Christ's church. Over the years, through serving the church in various roles—pastor, preacher, professor, administrator—our knowledge of and appreciation for the Wesleyan theological tradition has intensified.

What characteristics justify a book titled *Wesleyan Foundations for Evangelism*?

Let's examine Wesleyans from four perspectives: (1) church history, (2) relationship to Scripture, (3) doctrine, and (4) enthusiasm for mission.

THE WESLEYAN TRADITION HISTORICALLY

After the sixteenth-century Protestant Reformation, Protestantism divided into denominations and independent groups along theological and geographical lines. The process began quickly, with the conflict between Martin Luther (1483–1546) in Germany and Huldrych Zwingli (1484–1531) in Switzerland over the meaning of the Lord's Supper. Other divisions resulted from debates about God's sovereignty in Continental churches and the Church of England, and controversies over church government.

Where do Wesleyans fit into the Protestant panorama?

In 1534, Henry VIII (1491–1547), king of England, declared the English Church independent of the Roman Catholic Church. His primary reasons were both political and theological. Having produced no male heir, Henry appealed to Pope Clement VII (1478–1534) for an annulment of his marriage to Catherine of Aragon. He wanted to marry Anne Boleyn. Clement refused. On November 3, 1534, at Henry's urging, Parliament passed the first Act of Supremacy. This Act made Henry supreme head of the Church of England (Anglican), thus displacing the pope as head of the English Church and instilling theological and political power in the office of the monarch. In England, the office of the monarch would make the political decisions for the nation and also produce the church's prayer book, sermons, and official Bible, as in the King James Version of 1611.

Declaring the Church of England independent of Rome was one thing, establishing it as a church was quite another. For more than one hundred years, the Church of England would be graced by stellar theological creativity *and* plagued by bitter, often violent conflict.

Towering theological leaders included Thomas Cranmer (1489–1556)—archbishop of Canterbury and chief composer of the Book of Common Prayer, Matthew Parker (1504-75), Richard Hooker (1554–1600), and John Jewel (1522-71).

Conflict would include the five-year reign of Mary I (1516-58), during which the Roman Catholic Church was restored, persecution of Protestants became severe, and many Protestants fled for protection to Geneva, Switzerland. In other periods Catholics were persecuted.

The 1559 Elizabethan Settlement under Protestant Queen Elizabeth (1533–1603), in which the Catholics were deposed and the Church of England reinstated, established some lasting religious order.[1] Still, many "nonconformist" groups (also known as "dissenters" and "separatists") emerged; they rejected the established church. Nonconformists included Presbyterians, Puritans, Baptists, Free Churchmen, and Friends (Quakers).

The 1559 Elizabethan Settlement capped efforts to establish doctrinal order. But the church that emerged from the Settlement and the 1662 Act of Uniformity was neither strictly Protestant nor Roman Catholic.[2] The Anglican Church identifies itself as a *via media*, a "middle way" between Protestantism and Catholicism. Out of the period of conflict, the church embraced what it believed to be the best of the Protestant Reformers and the worldwide spirit of Catholicism. However, the Thirty-Nine Articles of Religion of the Church of England are clearly more Protestant than Catholic, especially Articles 6, 11-14, 22, 25, 28, and 32.[3]

Accepting the early confessions of the faith such as the Apostles' and Nicene Creeds, the Church of England is primarily defined by "how it prays." The Latin phrase Anglicans use to describe how they "do" theology is *Lex orandi, lex credendi*, which means "the rule of prayer [is] the rule of belief."[4] So instead of formal theological confessions, Anglicans have the Book of Common Prayer (they also have the Thirty-Nine Articles of Religion and the Book of Homilies[5]). What and how they *pray* is what they *believe*. Thanks largely to Thomas Cranmer, their prayers and Homilies are richly endowed with Scripture.[6] The designation "prayers" covers church services of reading Scripture and preaching, the rituals of baptism and the Eucharist, private prayers, and specific prayers for the nation and aid in spreading the gospel to all people in a variety of situations.

Wesleyan theology is rooted in the Church of England. The theology of John (1703-91) and Charles (1707-88) Wesley, founders of Methodism, was grounded in the Anglican *via media*, the Book of Common Prayer, the Thirty-Nine Articles of Religion, and the Book of Homilies. Until death, both were Anglican priests. They intended that Methodists would constitute an assembly *in* and *under* the ecclesiastical jurisdiction of the Church of England. But when independence came to the American colonies after the Revolutionary War, John reluctantly gave his blessing to American Methodists to become independent while writing an abbreviated Book of Common Prayer for the American Methodist movement. This happened formally in the 1784 Christmas Conference held in the Lovely Lane Chapel, Baltimore, Maryland. After John's death, Methodists in England formally separated from the Church of England. They became the Methodist Church of Great Britain.[7]

John and Charles Wesley largely adhered to the Thirty-Nine Articles of Religion. A notable exception is their rejection of Article 17, "Of Predestination and Election."[8] They taught instead that the atoning work of Jesus Christ is intended for all persons. They believed God's Word clearly teaches that Christ "is the atoning sacrifice for our sins, and not only for ours but also for the sins of the whole world" (1 John 2:2, NIV).[9] Their position had been clearly stated nine hundred years earlier by the Council of Quierzy (AD 853): "There is not, never has been, and never will be a single human being for whom Christ did not suffer." This remains the doctrinal standard of the Catholic Church.[10] It is also the theological guide for Methodists and often found in their writing and singing:

Come, sinners, to the gospel feast;
Let ev'ry soul be Jesus' guest.
Ye need not one be left behind,
For God hath bidden all mankind.[11]

John and Charles believed God's grace is "FREE IN ALL, and FREE FOR ALL."[12] John's text for his sermon "Free Grace" was Romans 8:32: "He that spared not his own Son, but delivered him up for us all, how shall he not with him also freely give us all things?" (KJV). Through prevenient grace the Holy Spirit works in all persons, seeking to lead them to salvation.[13]

So, with modifications, historically the Wesleyan lineage runs through the Church of England (Anglicanism) back to the Protestant Reformation. The doctrinal standards of Methodism and its daughter denominations reveal theological and linguistic dependence on the Thirty-Nine

Articles of Religion.[14] The Wesleyan tradition is also grounded in the great apostolic tradition as preserved in the Roman Catholic Church and Eastern Orthodoxy. Wesleyans are taught by, belong to, and contribute to the whole church.

THE WESLEYAN TRADITION AND SCRIPTURE

Characteristic of the Protestant Reformation were the "five *solas*": (1) *sola Scriptura* (Scripture alone), (2) *sola fide* (faith alone), (3) *sola gratia* (grace alone), (4) *solus Christus* (Christ alone), and (5) *soli Deo gloria* (to the glory of God alone). Protestantism placed the authority of Scripture above all councils and papal authority. Church tradition is subservient to Scripture.

Wesleyans affirm the "five *solas*." Their characteristic understanding of biblical authority is similar to John's statement in his Gospel: "These are written that you may believe that Jesus is the Messiah, the Son of God, and that by believing you may have life in his name" (20:30-31, NIV). John concentrated on those things that would most clearly reveal the Redeemer. Similarly, for Wesleyans the authority and principal importance of Scripture resides in its faithful and definitive testimony to how God is *for* and *with* his creation in Jesus Christ. In their statements about the Bible's authority, most Wesleyan denominations adhere to Article 6 of the Anglican Thirty Nine Articles of Religion, "Of the Sufficiency of the Holy Scripture for Salvation": "Holy Scripture containeth all things necessary to salvation: so that whatsoever is not read therein, nor may be proved thereby, is not to be required of any man, that it should be believed as an article of the Faith, or be thought requisite or necessary to salvation."[15] The Bible is fully sufficient in its declaration of "all things necessary"; that is its purpose. Its authority rests in its "sufficiency"—namely, its testimony to God's saving work in Christ. Culturally limited worldviews, for instance, found in the Bible are not "necessary to salvation" and are "not to be required" of anyone as an "article of the Faith."

Jesus Christ is the Word of God. The Bible is the Word of God secondarily, *as* faithful and definitive witness to Christ (Luke 24:25-27). The Bible's primary purpose is to lead persons to confess, by the Holy Spirit, that in Jesus Christ we encounter God the Redeemer, "the Lamb of God, who takes away the sin of the world" (John 1:29, NIV). Therein rests its binding authority.

The Bible remains a closed book until opened by the Holy Spirit. Just as "no one can say, 'Jesus is Lord,' except by the Holy Spirit" (1 Cor. 12:3, NIV), even so, only the Holy Spirit can transform the Bible into Scripture, into a living witness to the "Word of God" (2:6-16).

Wesleyan New Testament scholar Joel B. Green takes the topic a step further. "The authority of Scripture," he says, "is best discerned in the lives (and not only the claims) of communities oriented around Scripture."[16] That is where and how the trustworthiness or "truth" of the Bible is confirmed. Green is echoing John Wesley, who preached that as important as doctrine is, true religion doesn't primarily reside there. John Wesley taught that true religion doesn't end with right doctrine (*orthodoxy*). It must result in *orthokardia* ("right heart" or "passions" or "values") and *orthopraxy* ("right action").

Wesleyans study the Scriptures diligently to learn how to live as faithful citizens in God's kingdom. Authoritative in all things that pertain to salvation, the Bible's moral norms faithfully express God's holy character and his will for his people.

In the preface to his *Sermons on Several Occasions*, John Wesley said, "At any price, give me the book of God! I have it: Here is knowledge enough for me. Let me be *homo unius libri* [a man of one book]."[17] However, Wesley stressed the importance of other books for Christian nurture and learning. For the education of Methodists, Wesley produced a "Christian library." The 1821 edition contained thirty volumes, with works on the Scriptures, testimonies, church histories, and theology.[18]

Wesleyans must heed a lesson from the Pharisees, who trumpeted their fidelity to the law of Moses. Jesus rebuked them for undercutting the Torah by elevating their rules above its spirit (Matt. 23:1-36). Similarly, denominations can boldly declare *sola Scriptura* while in practice placing their own cherished doctrines beyond the reach of biblical critique. To be truly Wesleyan, each identifying doctrine must regularly be subjected to examination and refinement by the Word of God.

All this means that Wesleyans are primarily children and servants of the triune God revealed in Jesus Christ by the will of the Father and the faithful witness of the Holy Spirit. Only secondarily are they loyal to their theological tradition, always engaged in "increasing in the knowledge of God" (Col. 1:10, KJV).

THE WESLEYAN TRADITION THEOLOGICALLY

All orthodox denominations have their distinctive characteristics. However, all must submit to judgment by *catholic* or universal doctrinal norms. An exhaustive examination of those norms is beyond this chapter. But we will identify four essential bases for Christian orthodoxy: (1) early creeds in the New Testament, (2) the Apostles' Creed, (3) the AD 325 Nicene Creed (Nicene-Constantinople Creed), and (4) the AD 451 Creed of Chalcedon. We will ask how Wesleyans measure up.

When we speak of Christian creeds, we mean the living faith of the church, carefully stated and embodied in practice (Rom. 10:9-11). *Credo* means "I believe."

First, Early Creeds of the New Testament

Broadly understood, the entire New Testament is a confession of faith that Jesus Christ is the Messiah of God. Before the close of the New Testament era, Christians were summarizing this faith in compact ways.

- Romans 1:2-4 (RSV). At the beginning of his letter to the church in Rome, the apostle Paul stated the gospel he preached everywhere. Through the prophets, God "promised beforehand . . . in the holy scriptures, the gospel concerning his Son, who was descended from David according to the flesh and designated Son of God in power according to the Spirit of holiness by his resurrection from the dead, Jesus Christ our Lord."
- 1 Corinthians 11:23-26 (RSV). Here Paul wrote the church about the Lord's Supper or Eucharist (thanksgiving). Paul "received from the Lord" instruction about this sacrament. This indicates that the early church had already placed the Lord's Supper at the center of its faith. The body and blood of Jesus the Messiah, shed on the cross, along with an expectation that Christ will return in glory, forms the center of the new covenant.

  For I received from the Lord what I also delivered to you, that the Lord Jesus on the night when he was betrayed took bread,

> and when he had given thanks, he broke it, and said, "This is my body which is for you. Do this in remembrance of me." In the same way also the cup, after supper, saying, "This cup is the new covenant in my blood. Do this, as often as you drink it, in remembrance of me." For as often as you eat this bread and drink the cup, you proclaim the Lord's death until he comes.

For Wesleyans, the Eucharist as the gospel of God, received by faith, is central to their faith. They do not claim to know *how* Christ is present in the Eucharist, but they know by the Holy Spirit their ascended Redeemer *is* present as their spiritual food and drink. With Charles Wesley they affirm,

Here all Thy blessings we receive,
Here all Thy gifts are given,
To those that would in Thee believe,
Pardon, and grace, and heaven.
Thus may we still in Thee be blest,
Till all from earth remove,
And share with Thee the marriage feast,
And drink the wine above.[19]

- 1 Corinthians 15:3-8 (NIV). Christianity is an Easter faith or nothing at all. Had the Father not raised Jesus from the grave, the gospel would be a lie (vv. 12-20). Paul expresses the church's Easter faith:

> For what I received I passed on to you as of first importance: that Christ died for our sins according to the Scriptures, that he was buried, that he was raised on the third day according to the Scriptures, and that he appeared to Cephas, and then to the Twelve. After that, he appeared to more than five hundred of the brothers and sisters at the same time, most of whom are still living, though some have fallen asleep. Then he appeared to James, then to all the apostles, and last of all he appeared to me also, as to one abnormally born. (Vv. 3-8)

- Philippians 2:6-11 (RSV). The "kenotic" (self-emptying) affirmation of Christian faith appears in the form of an early hymn.[20] It is Paul's "master story."[21] In it we encounter the essential nature of the triune God, who freely gives himself to redeem sinful humankind. The passage not only tells us about the incarnation but also "is a new understanding of God."[22] God is self-emptying. The hymn tells of the willing incarnation of the Son of God, his servanthood in full human form, his obedient death on the cross, his resurrection, his exaltation, and his final manifestation as Lord of Lords and King of Kings.

> Though he was in the form of God, [he] did not count equality with God a thing to be grasped, but emptied himself, taking the form of a servant, being born in the likeness of men. And being found in human form he humbled himself and became obedient unto death, even death on a cross. Therefore God has highly exalted him and bestowed on him the name which is above every name, that at the name of Jesus every knee should bow, in heaven and on earth and under the earth, and every tongue confess that Jesus Christ is Lord, to the glory of God the Father.

- 1 Timothy 3:16 (RSV). The New Testament's most succinct confession of faith is the six-part affirmation in 1 Timothy.

> Great indeed, we confess, is the mystery of our religion:
> He was manifested in the flesh,
> vindicated in the Spirit,
> seen by angels,
> preached among the nations,
> believed on in the world,
> taken up in glory.

The gospel John Wesley proclaimed was "that faith which the Apostles themselves had while our Lord was on earth." It "acknowledges the necessity and merit of Christ's death, and the power of his resurrection. It acknowledges his death as the only sufficient means of redeeming man from death eternal, and his resurrection as the restoration of us all to life and immortality."[23] Wesleyans affirm each part of the preceding creedal statements.

Second, the Apostles' Creed

Wesleyans do not have a formal institutional "creed" of their own as do some Protestant churches. They affirm, without equivocation, the great creeds formulated during what John Wesley called "primitive and apostolical" Christianity.[24] His emphasis upon a heart warmed by the transforming Holy Spirit should never be confused with doctrinal negligence or relativism. Wesleyan theologian David F. Watson says John Wesley "assumed the truth of the church's great Creeds and he assumed other Christians did as well."[25] A truly "catholic Christian," Wesley taught, "is fixed as the sun in his judgment concerning the main branches of Christian doctrine."[26] The great creeds of Christendom buttress the "grand scheme of doctrine"[27] found in the Scriptures.

The Apostles' Creed is a universal confession of Christian faith. Its origins are not precisely known, but it was in use in the church by the time of the writing of the Gospels. Its name derives from a legend that it was written by the apostles on the day of Pentecost, each apostle contributing one article. The creed was used as a catechism to prepare new Christians for baptism as their witness to the faith believed by all Christians in all places. In its present form the creed probably derives from the third century. Its original form goes back to the Old Roman Creed. It might have achieved its final form as late as the seventh century. Once formulated, the creed spread throughout the church as the basic form of its faith. In some parts of the church the creed continues to form part of the liturgy for baptism.[28]

The Apostles' Creed has twelve articles or sections.[29] Wesleyans affirm each article without reservation.

- I believe in God, the Father almighty, creator of heaven and earth.
- I believe in Jesus Christ, his only Son, our Lord.
- He was conceived by the power of the Holy Spirit and born of the Virgin Mary.
- He suffered under Pontius Pilate, was crucified, died, and was buried.
- He descended to the dead. On the third day he rose again.
- He ascended into heaven, and is seated at the right hand of the Father.
- He will come again to judge the living and the dead.
- I believe in the Holy Spirit,
- the holy catholic Church, the communion of saints,

- the forgiveness of sins,
- the resurrection of the body,
- and the life everlasting. Amen.[30]

Third, the Nicene Creed (AD 325)

Early in the fourth century a theological dispute erupted in Alexandria, Egypt, between a presbyter (priest) named Arius (ca. AD 256–336) and his bishop, Alexander (ca. AD 312-ca. AD 328). The dispute would lead to the church's first ecumenical council, to decades of theological conflict, and to churches that followed the teaching of Arius. Held in high regard as a preacher, Arius taught that the Son of God, who became incarnate in Jesus of Nazareth, was not God as the Father is God—not of the same essence. Instead, the Son was the Father's first creation—the first born of creation—through whom the rest of creation came to be. The Father, who is eternal, has no beginning; but as created, the Son does. To Arius's credit, he was trying to protect the absolute unity of God (monotheism) against the polytheism (multiple gods) characteristic of Greco-Roman culture. But his efforts came at the deadly price of denying the Redeemer is God. The logic of the Nicene Creed remains our standard of faith. Only God, the one who is truly fully God, can save. If Jesus is not fully God, then he cannot save us. Therefore, the church affirms in the Nicene Creed that Jesus Christ is fully God, begotten and not made, sharing the same substance and being with the Father. Jesus saves.

The controversy burned like wildfire in the Eastern (Greek) part of the church and threatened to split Christianity just after Emperor Constantine had embraced the Christian faith and elevated Christianity to a legal religion within the Roman Empire. It led to the first general (ecumenical) church council, which met in the town of Nicaea[31] in AD 325. The majority of the approximately 318 convening bishops concluded that the Son is of the same substance or essence as the Father. The council adopted the Greek term *homo-ousia* (same substance) and rejected an alternative possibility that would have declared the Son to be of "similar essence or substance" (*homoi-ousia*) with the Father.

Today, in the Nicene Creed all orthodox Christians confess that God is one. They also confess "one Lord, Jesus Christ, . . . eternally begotten of the Father, . . . true God from true God, begotten, not made, of one Being with the Father." They also confess the church is "one holy catholic and apostolic," with faith in the one Lord.[32] These are the four "marks" of the church. When Christians affirm the church is holy, they don't mean it is flawless but that Christ's redeeming and sanctifying presence resides in it, making of it "a dwelling place of God" (Eph. 2:19-22, RSV) and equipping it as "salt of the earth" and a light to the world (Matt. 5:13-16, RSV).

The Nicene Creed of 325 affirmed "and in the Holy Spirit" as part of what the church believes. But it did not clearly affirm the full deity of the Holy Spirit. That deficit was corrected in AD 381 in the Council of Constantinople, the second ecumenical council. It consisted of 150 bishops (all from the East).[33] This council affirmed the deity of the Holy Spirit as part of the Trinity with the Father and the Son: "We believe in the Holy Spirit, the Lord, the giver of life, who proceeds from the Father and the Son [added later by the Latin Church]. With the Father and the Son he is worshiped and glorified."[34]

So the Nicene Creed Christians confess today is actually the Nicene-Constantinople Creed, commonly shortened to the Nicene Creed.[35] Nicaea and Constantinople spelled out with clarity what the New Testament repeatedly affirms. So orthodox Christians are Trinitarian monotheists—one God in three persons—Father, Son, and Holy Spirit. The essential parts of the doctrine of the Trinity were in place. But it would require more time for the church to show how best to articulate Trinitarian life.

With all orthodox Christians, Wesleyans affirm the Nicene Creed. In John Wesley's 1784 abridgment of the Thirty-Nine Articles of Religion, Article 1 is "Of Faith in the Holy Trinity": "And in unity of this Godhead there are three persons, of one substance, power, and eternity—the Father, the Son, and the Holy Ghost."[36]

Fourth, the Creed of Chalcedon

The Council of Nicaea settled the question about the eternal, preexistent Godhead of Christ. But it did not address an equally important topic: Christ's humanity. The central paradox of the Christian faith is that the eternal God became fully incarnate in the equally fully human person

Jesus of Nazareth. But how was the church to explain how Jesus could remain fully human while all the fullness of God was pleased to dwell in him (Col. 1:19; John 1:1)?

Numerous Christian thinkers who affirmed Nicaea and Constantinople tried unsuccessfully to answer the question. Two of these attempts occasioned the Council of Chalcedon in AD 451.[37] The council reaffirmed the Nicene Creed and established the orthodox way of expressing our Lord's humanity in relationship to his deity.

Wisely, the Council of Chalcedon did not try to offer a rational explanation for how Christ's two natures—divine and human—reside complete in one undivided person. The mystery of the incarnation is a confession of obedient faith. Chalcedon affirmed what *must be true* of the Redeemer and *how* the mystery can be explained as consistent with the Scriptures. As is true of the incarnation, the Creed of Chalcedon is suprarational but not irrational, offering the explanation of the mystery of Christ according to the church's confession of faith in the Scriptures.

The creed affirms Christ is "perfect in Godhead and also perfect in manhood; truly God and truly man, of a rational soul and body; coessential [same divine essence] with the Father according to the Godhead, and consubstantial [of the same nature] with us according to the manhood; in all things like unto us, without sin." Christ is to be "acknowledged in two natures, without confusion, without change, without division, without separation; the distinction of natures being by no means taken away by the union, but rather the property of each nature being preserved, and concurring in one person."[38]

Philip Schaff says Chalcedon means "the whole work of Christ is to be attributed to his person, and not to the one or the other nature exclusively."[39] The importance of Chalcedon is that "it substantially completes the orthodox Christology of the ancient Church."[40] It is this firm belief that underlies the Wesleyan enthusiasm for mission and evangelism.

THE WESLEYAN TRADITION AND MISSION

A "profound gratitude to God and a deep compassion for others" propelled John and Charles Wesley. They had "received a message that made all the difference in their own lives," and they gave themselves in sermon and song to "sharing that message with others in the hope it would transform their lives as well."[41] They were servants of the *missio Dei*, the mission of God.

When speaking of the mission of the church, we first speak of the *missio Dei.* The church's mission is defined and fulfilled by its faithfulness to God's mission, which Wesleyan New Testament scholar Andy Johnson defines as bringing God's "creation to its full potential and to do[ing] so through the agency of humanity."[42] Its very nature is mission; in its whole being and in all its members, the church is sent to announce, bear witness to, and make present the revelation of the triune God in Jesus Christ, "in whom we have redemption through his blood" (Eph. 1:7, KJV). Paul says that in Christ, God has made known to his church "the mystery of his will, according to his purpose which he set forth in Christ as a plan for the fullness of time, to unite all things in him, things in heaven and things on earth" (vv. 9-10, RSV). This is the redemptive action of the "missionary God," constituting, sanctifying, and empowering his "missionary church." In his church, visible but endowed with invisible graces, Christ fulfills and reveals his own mystery, the embodiment (1 Cor. 12:12-14; Eph. 5:30-32) of God's eternal plan (Eph. 1:9-10).

The missional God became fully incarnate in Jesus of Nazareth. By the power of the Holy Spirit, Jesus obeyed his Father's will, even to death on the cross (Phil. 2:8). Being the expressed "image" (Gk., *eikōn*, "likeness") of the invisible God (Col. 1:15), Christ fully revealed his heavenly Father (John 10:30; 14:9). In the Gospel of John, Jesus identifies himself as the "I AM" who spoke to Moses from the burning bush (Exod. 3:13-15, NIV).[43] Jesus fulfilled all the Scriptures of promise. And he gathered about himself an unlikely band of disciples, the core of the new and true Israel. As promised, at Pentecost the Holy Spirit came upon the disciples in power, took up his abode in them, and made of them agents of God's mission in the world. They were to embody God's will and declare him among the nations. They were to faithfully mediate to the world God's love, will, and glory (Phil. 1:9-11). What began at Pentecost continues in the members of Christ's church, servants of the Great Commission.[44]

Wesleyan theologian Phil Meadows says the *missio Dei* is "fundamentally what God does to lead humanity through the whole way of salvation—by setting us free from sin, filling us with the divine life, and renewing us in holy love."[45] The mission of the triune God is to reveal or declare himself in creative and redemptive glory and love and to create a covenant people who will faithfully reflect God *in* and *to* his creation. The purpose of the creation, says Joseph Ratzinger, is to "open up a space for response to God's love, to his holy will."[46]

Meadows identifies two dimensions as it relates to God's coworkers. "First, we become coworkers with God as *recipients* of the *missio Dei*, when we are caught up in the missional flow of God's prevenient, justifying, and sanctifying grace."[47] "Second, we are coworkers with God as *participants* in the *missio Dei*, when the love and grace we have received reaches out to others in a life of witness and service."[48] To borrow from New Testament scholar N. T. Wright, as heralds of God's new creation inaugurated in the cross of Christ, Jesus now sends his witness into the world as "rescued rescuers, justified justice-bringers, reconciled reconcilers, and the new Passover People."[49]

Jesus's High Priestly Prayer (John 17:1-26) maps the *missio Dei*. *First*, Jesus prays for himself. *Second*, he prays for the apostles. *Third*, he prays for all who will believe in him through the apostles' word. In Jesus's prayer, there is a *triple sanctification* (vv. 17-19), each of which is integral to the mission of God. In the strictest sense, sanctity or holiness belongs to God alone; it uniquely marks his singularity as God. But he can claim a person or thing for his purpose and so make them holy by association. Therefore, the verb "sanctify" (Hebr., *qādaš*, "make holy," "consecrate," "set apart for God"; Gk., *hagiazo*, "to purify," "make holy," "consecrate") means completely "handing over" or "consecrating" a person or thing to God as a vehicle of worship and service (Rom. 12:1). What is sanctified is not only *for God* but also *for the world* on God's behalf, for its healing and reconciliation with God.

Consider the three "sanctifications" in John 17:17-19 as they relate to "mission." In the *first*, the Father sanctifies his Son—consecrates him to his own will—and sends him into the world for the healing of the nations. Jesus is joined to his Father in unbroken obedience and to the world in redemptive mission.

In the *second* sanctification, the Son *offers* himself to the Father's will. "Here I am, I have come to do your will" (Heb. 10:9, NIV). Jesus prayed, “Not as I will, but as thou wilt” (Matt. 26:39, RSV). This is the unbroken pattern of Jesus’s life and ministry. Through his sufferings Jesus “learned obedience” and was thus “made perfect” (Gk., *teleiōtheis*, “complete”; Heb. 5:8-9).[50] His yes to the Father “consecrated” (sanctified) him to “become a merciful and faithful high priest” (2:17, RSV).

Third, on the basis of and in conformity with Jesus’s own sanctification, he prays that all his disciples be sanctified “in the truth” (John 17:17, RSV). Jesus draws them into his own sanctification, into his and his Father’s own life and mission. The church’s sanctification for mission is grounded in and provided by Jesus’s own consecration, his own sanctification. The apostle Paul says this is the meaning of Christian baptism. In baptism the old self “lived” in opposition to sanctification “dies,” just as surely as Christ died on the cross. By God’s resurrecting power, a new “self” comes to new life in the Spirit. Now, “to live is Christ, and to die is gain” (Phil. 1:21, RSV). Christian sanctification means living out our baptism into Christ, by the Spirit’s power (Rom. 8:1-5) in all dimensions of life. Paul states it plainly: “No longer present your members to sin as instruments of wickedness, but present yourselves to God as those who have been brought from death to life, and present your members to God as instruments of righteousness” (6:13, NRSV). Resurrection life is sanctified life (vv. 5-8), the answer to Jesus’s High Priestly Prayer (John 17:17-19).

Sanctification is about becoming thoroughly equipped for obedient, worshipful mission. It means being “filled with the fruit of righteousness that comes through Jesus Christ—to the glory and praise of God” (Phil. 1:11, NIV). Sanctification certainly includes the individual. But its chief end is to glorify God in all things, just as in Christ’s obedience he glorified his Father. Correctly understood, this is what “entire sanctification” means in the Wesleyan tradition; it is loving, practiced confidence and life in the sanctified Christ, who by the Holy Spirit sanctifies his church (1 Cor. 1:2) for God’s own mission and glory (Rom. 12:1; Eph. 1:6).

It is this positive understanding of mission—combined with the Wesleyan adherence to the apostolic faith—that is the catalyst for our beliefs about and attempts at sharing Christ with the whole world. The following chapters explore, in more detail, how these foundations should guide Wesleyans in evangelism.

Questions for Consideration

1. Why is grounding in Christian doctrine essential for evangelism?
2. What is there about the Wesleyan tradition that prepares it as a vehicle for evangelism?
3. Why is it essential to speak of a "missional God" before speaking of a "missional people"?

Additional Resources

Crutcher, Timothy J. *John Wesley: His Life and Thought.* Kansas City: Beacon Hill Press of Kansas City, 2015.

Green, Richard. *John Wesley: Evangelist.* London: Religious Tract Society, 1905. Wesley Center Online. http://wesley.nnu.edu/john-wesley/john-wesley-evangelist/.

Johnson, Andy. *Holiness and the Missio Dei.* Eugene, OR: Cascade Books, 2016.

Knight, Henry H., III, and F. Douglas Powe Jr. *Transforming Evangelism: The Wesleyan Way of Sharing Faith.* Nashville: Discipleship Resources, 2006.

Maddox, Randy L. *Responsible Grace: John Wesley's Practical Theology.* Nashville: Abingdon, 1994.

Witherington, Ben. "Why a Wesleyan Approach to Theology: Seven-Minute Seminary." Published on April 10, 2013. Seedbed video, 6:41. https://www.youtube.com/watch?v=6sG08YuAZEU.

2

THE GREAT COMMISSION IN A POSTMODERN AND PLURALISTIC WORLD

Carla Sunberg, PhD

We met casually over the ordinary and mundane, our lives having no shared history. Here I am, a grandmother whose world has often been defined by the Berlin Wall and the Soviet Union. I was raised in the era of the Cold War, the "hangover" the world lived with after the Second World War. The last century saw humanity wrestle with modernism and its search for truth, as witnessed by political debates and shoe banging at the United Nations by a Russian dictator.[1] In the end the world somehow survived without blowing itself up. And yet, those of us who are children of that era still wrestle with modern boundaries that largely define us.

Brianna, my acquaintance, had experienced none of this, having been raised in a rural community in the Midwest. Her struggle was how to break from the traditions of home. Those included her Roman Catholic heritage and the family farm. None of these held any interest for her. So she left to find adventure in the big city. Having shed the traditions of her past, she's now a free spirit—sweet, lovely, and hoping to find beneficial relationships and peace. Together we struggle to find common ground in our conversations. Somehow we have found a place where we can each share our story.

We live in a time when much of the Western world is experiencing a cosmic collision between ideology and life experience. For many, shifting from modernism to postmodernism makes it difficult to keep up. Some of us find ourselves holding on to the past, white-knuckled, scared to death to let go because we don't want to be swept away by something we find hard to understand. We want the world to remain the same; the new ways people are thinking make many of us uncomfortable.

The church is not excluded from this seismic shift in thought about our world. But before we conclude the changes are too demanding for the church, we ought to remember Jesus's words, "I will build my church" (Matt. 16:18, NIV). This is the Lord's church, not ours. If we live in fear of the times, we are not trusting the living God. French Protestant reformer Theodore Beza (1519–1605) told Jeanne of Navarre in 1561, "It belongs to the church of God to receive blows rather than to inflict them—but, she is an anvil that has worn out many hammers."[2] This is not the first time the church has had to adjust to a changing culture, and it won't be the last. Instead of fearing what lies ahead, we must learn to rely upon God and trust that he is at the helm!

In recent years it seems as if evangelism has disappeared from center stage in much of the church. I've heard people say the Great Commission (Matt. 28:16-20) has become the Great Suggestion. Numerous reasons lie behind this, specifically, much that is wrapped up in postmodernity. To understand the reaction to evangelism, we need to understand something of what postmodernism means.

As the term indicates, "postmodernity" identifies the historical era that succeeds modernity. It is largely a rejection of much that characterized modernity. One rejected feature is the belief that through the right use of reason, moral, political, and social norms can be established for beneficially organizing society worldwide. Postmodernists reject that belief as "oppressive" and disrespectful of diverse cultures and worldviews. Supposed universal claims about "truth" must be "deconstructed." There is no uniform agreement about when postmodernity emerged or even what it all means.[3]

When postmodernism began appearing in the late twentieth century, there were those who decried it as something to avoid at all costs. This, however, would amount to avoiding the air we breathe. Postmodernity is not something to avoid; it is simply the time in which we live. Understandably, for those still rooted in modernity, the times can be disorienting. We should remember the reaction is against the modernity of the last century that nearly had us blowing up the world. Now, a new generation is rising that is unhappy about how modernity played out. They believe there are better ways for humans to flourish.

IN LIGHT OF POSTMODERNITY

In search of something better than what modernity offered, postmodern people began to challenge the modern notion that through a right use of reason humans can find and define universal religious and political truth for everyone. Postmodern thinkers see the modern effort toward universality as a great failure. The effort, they insist, nearly destroyed the world. Postmodernists refuse to be placed into rigid categories, whether religious or ideological.[4] Instead, barriers between people are to be removed and truth is to be defined by one's own perception of reality. Understandingly, for many, postmodernity is very disconcerting.

Enter tolerance. In the last century humans became intolerant of those judged to be different. For example, early in the twentieth century the Ottoman Empire engaged in Armenian genocide. Armenians were different; they were of a peculiar religion (Christianity), and they were a "problem" for the Ottomans. Later, Nazis saw Jews as a problem in need of a "final solution." Viewing Jews as social parasites, the Nazis planned and tried to carry out their extermination in what we know as the horrific holocaust. Meanwhile, the Soviet Union lost millions of people in battles on its frontiers. Millions more died in Russia at the hands of their own leaders because of ideological conflicts. Before the century was over, homosexuals in England were imprisoned and chemically castrated. During World War II,

Japanese in the United States were placed in internment camps when it was feared they would become traitors against their new homeland. Battles over civil rights scarred the face of the United States, while Apartheid was creating a hellish environment for people of South Africa separated by race.

Postmodernists say "No!" to the kind of intolerance witnessed in the last century. They insist on peace, love, and tolerance! Interestingly, at times there can be an almost violent reaction against those viewed as intolerant of another's definition of truth.

Materialism is defined in the postmodern context quite differently from the way it was in the modern era. While modernity encouraged technological development, consumerism, and materialism, postmodern people see the material world differently. This results in a different understanding of materialism. Postmodernists shun twentieth-century consumerist materialism. Instead, the natural order is found in mother earth, with a resultant championing of long-term care for the material world.

Often in the past century a holiness lifestyle was defined by not drinking, dancing, or smoking, while nevertheless driving large gas-guzzling vehicles, building luxurious homes, and overeating until being a Christian almost became synonymous with obesity. With the long view in mind, postmodern Christians view a holiness lifestyle as synonymous with care for each other, for the earth, and for future generations. Decisions about food, vehicles, the use of plastics, and the well-being of others above oneself are urgent values.

A young man seated next to me on the plane was David. He wanted to chat. I wasn't sure I wanted to talk, but I thought I ought to follow his lead in the conversation. He was sixteen years old and was on his way to spend time with his grandmother in Kansas. He was dressed in black and wore a unique necklace. Something that looked a bit like a satanic symbol hung from it. We talked about marching bands, something we had in common (albeit, for me, many years ago). We talked about what Kansas is like in the fall. Then he told me that he was deeply spiritual and that he spent a lot of time walking and meditating. He mentioned his necklace; he said it wasn't anything evil, just spiritual. But everything he talked about seemed dark; the places where he was seeking spirituality were somewhat frightening to me. I asked if he'd ever been to church. No, never in his entire life. He didn't really know anything about Christianity and didn't seem to think it was an option for his spiritual needs. I gave him my personal information and told him I'd be available to talk about a "brighter side" of spirituality if ever he was interested.

FROM THE MODERN

We modernists of the last century tried hard to codify spirituality. We created boxes to define ourselves and plans for presenting the gospel to others. Some German and American schools of theology and philosophy turned spirituality into a scientific experiment for intellectual dissection until there was almost no space left for the mystery of God. But humans are created as spiritual beings, not as objects for scientific dissection. Witness the great hunger for spirituality pouring from our young people. Sadly, too often the church, living in a modern box, cannot provide a way to feed their spiritual hunger.

So far, I have given a modernist viewpoint of postmodernism. That's my "social location."[5] I find it difficult to refrain from trying to place things in categories. Please forgive me. The fact is that all of us are living in a time of great transition. Most of us find ourselves somewhere on the continuum running from modernity to postmodernity, and it can be destabilizing. It presses us to examine how we have done things in the past and then look toward the future. While radically different, the changed context is ripe with possibility.

Modernity was a generator of programs. The church itself became enthralled by one program after another. By programs we were going to teach ourselves the "what and the how" of ministry, including evangelism. We would memorize and practice formulas for success. Evangelism often became largely a method for reaching candidates for Christian conversion. Methods are not to be discounted; we just must make sure they are not primary and that they serve the correct purpose. They are not food for the soul of a postmodern world. I believe an overemphasis on method is one reason evangelism has largely disappeared from our vocabulary.

In a postmodern world that insists on tolerance, it's tempting for the church to yield to the belief that whatever one identifies as religious and moral truth should be accepted. This is the contemporary context of pluralism the church faces.

SUGGESTION OR COMMISSION

All this might leave us wondering if there is a future for evangelism. What should we now do with the Great Commission in a world that insists on religious tolerance? In the future it is best to abandon counterproductive approaches to the Great Commission and recover *an ancient-future pathway*. This includes looking to the early church to find a way forward.

First, we must examine *why* we engage in evangelism. Is it to increase church membership? Is it because we are pressured to approach strangers and talk with them about Jesus? Are we just trying to make converts for our denomination? If we find ourselves answering yes to these questions, then we are trapped in a modern mentality from which we need to be set free.

The first Christian evangelist was Mary with whom Jesus spoke on the morning of his resurrection:

> Jesus said to her, "Do not hold on to me, because I have not yet ascended to the Father. But go to my brothers and say to them, 'I am ascending to my Father and your Father, to my God and your God.'"
>
> Mary Magdalene went and announced to the disciples, "I have seen the Lord"; and she told them that he had said these things to her. (John 20:17-18, NRSV)

Mary ran to tell the others the good news; she had "seen the Lord." Mary teaches us that to be an evangelist means sharing the good news. It doesn't mean converting someone to your way of thinking. Jesus told his followers to go and "make disciples" (Matt. 28:19, NRSV). Sharing the "good news" and "making disciples" have two prerequisites. *First*, you must have some good news to share. *Second*, you need to be a disciple of Jesus yourself. Could it be that our overly programmed or routine ways of "being church" have left us without a story to tell? Without an urgent story to tell, tools, techniques, and programs displace the good news. To be truly Christian, evangelism must begin in our own lives as Jesus's disciples. There is no substitute for *our own story* of Jesus as our Redeemer.

A heart filled with love for Christ is commissioned to share good news because such news cannot be restrained.

A few years ago, while we were living in Russia, my husband, Chuck, was leading a Bible Study for a group of people who were not Christians. They were simply interested, wanting to learn more about the Bible and what Christians believe. By reading through the Beatitudes, Chuck was explaining Jesus's beautiful Sermon on the Mount. One night as he was completing the study, one of the men asked, "Do you live like that?" My husband asked, "What do you mean?" He responded, "You're the only Christian we've ever met, and you're telling us what Jesus said we should do. We just want to know if you live that way." Returning home that evening, Chuck was a bit stunned.

Our lives are supposed to be living witnesses to the good news of Jesus Christ. If we are the only Christians, someone ever sees, we should pray that he or she will see Christ in us. The story of Jesus and the good news has power only when it is authentic. We can't be Christians only on Sundays[6] and think we can effectively share the good news. What if you are the first Christian someone meets? Will he or she want to live like you?

While writing this chapter, I was in Africa. I was changing planes in Addis Ababa, Ethiopia. As I was waiting for my flight, I noticed a sign pointing to a prayer room. There, in the middle of the day, was a Muslim man on his knees in prayer. Muslims pray five times daily (*salat*). They are serious about their faith, and it is obvious. By contrast, many Christians hardly pray publicly for their food anymore. For the world to believe we have good news to tell, we must be authentic. Jesus's disciples must faithfully reflect him in the world.

This is where we find the hope for evangelism—reflecting Christ in the world. In a postmodern environment, where everyone can define truth for themselves, we have an opportunity to reflect, bear witness to, Jesus who is Truth (John 14:6). The focus of our lives and the ministry of the church must be Jesus. We should be teaching about Jesus, discipling one another to become more like him and allowing Jesus to inform all our actions and reactions.

As Wesleyan-Holiness people, we should be in the middle of the postmodern conversation, not denying or fleeing from it. We are in a good position because we believe the gospel of Jesus Christ is for everyone, and we know the Holy Spirit is graciously operative in all persons, whatever the era or context. As partners in the Spirit's work, we should reach out to others with a hand of holy love. We should find creative ways to be channels of prevenient grace. The holiness message we hold dear should always be defined in relation to Christ and as servants of triune life. We must be constantly transformed by God's abounding grace. True, God's grace is "lavished" (Eph. 1:7-8, NRSV) upon those who follow Christ. But God's grace and love are also to be shared with all those with whom we come in contact (3:9). Paul even includes announcing the gospel to "principalities and powers" (v. 10, KJV). Through the Holy Spirit we become Christ bearers in the world, taking him and the good news of the Truth wherever we go.

PLURALISM

But is the world in need of this truth, in need of Jesus, who is "the way, the truth, and the life" (John 14:6, KJV)? The question raises the topic of religious pluralism. Central to a postmodern worldview is that there is no universal master story, no metanarrative applicable to all persons and cultures. Here we encounter a tension. Respect for pluralism is an essential feature of a postmodern world seeking individual love and peace. Pluralism is "a state of society in which members of diverse ethnic, racial, religious, or social groups maintain and develop their traditional culture or special interest within the confines of a common civilization."[7] Living peacefully in diverse cultures should be attractive to all Christians. On that basis, some have argued that "evangelism" and "pluralism" are mutually exclusive. If you respect another person's "space," you will not engage in evangelism. The accusation is that "evangelism is arrogant and imperialist, oppressive." It is "totally inappropriate in a pluralist society."[8]

Anglican theologian Alister McGrath warns the church that this is a shallow and destructive response. The church has always lived in a pluralistic world. However, McGrath recognizes that according to the postmodern mood, "claims by any one group or individual to have any exclusive hold on 'truth' are thus treated as the intellectual equivalent of fascism."[9] If this were true, it would reject the New Testament claim that "grace and truth came through Jesus Christ" (John 1:17, NRSV). Pluralism appears to leave Christians and the church in a quandary. On the one hand, we want to show love and respect for others. On the other hand, we are commissioned to declare that Jesus Christ is "the way, the truth, and the life" for all people (John 14:6, KJV).

Let me return for a moment to Africa, where we continue to learn lessons about the revelation of Jesus as the Light of the World. During a gathering of believers, I sip tea and listen to the stories of former Muslims who are now Jesus's disciples. As noted earlier, according to modern models we must have a program, a plan, or *strategy* if we expect to "win" people to Christ. But the stories told by these men are full of much more mystery. A young Muslim kneeling during daily prayers, crying out to God to know truth, suddenly looks to his right, and there is Jesus, in the mosque, kneeling beside him! Others tell similar stories of Jesus appearing and revealing himself to them.[10] Jesus himself opened their eyes to the Truth. You see, everything points to Jesus, not primarily to carefully planned strategies. Either he will reveal himself directly or be reflected in the lives of his followers. Our responsibility is simply to bear witness to him in the world. Through the Holy Spirit, Jesus himself will "convince" without in any way disrespecting "context." None of the men I heard speaking thought their "space" had been violated by Jesus. The Truth is liberating, not oppressive.

In a pluralistic world, we value dialogue with those who might not agree with us. We walk with respect for others, not trying to convert by any form of trickery or coercion. We are willing to have honest and authentic conversation, taking the risk that about many things the other person just might be correct. Dialogue can used by the Holy Spirit and can result in change. Alister McGrath says this posture "lies at the heart of responsible Christian evangelism—that the inner truth of Christianity has a power to convert. Evangelism is in no way inconsistent with respect for others."[11] The revelation of Christ through the Spirit's witness, whether through proclamation, our lives, or conversation, is what holds the power to transform lives.

DIALOGUE AND INVITATION

Too often we are ready to point out where someone needs to change because of what we think he or she is doing wrong. We can't help it. As modern people we've been culturally "programmed" to think that way. Changing that disposition can happen with the practice of patience and through prayer. May God help us to have a heart that focuses on expressing God's love and showing hospitality, instead of beginning with what may be perceived as intolerance. This doesn't mean Christians must abandon primary convictions about Christ and the gospel the church has held for two thousand years. But it does mean intentionally starting with an overflow of holy love that might open the door for sharing the good news of Jesus Christ.

For everyone there is mystery involved in coming to Christ (Eph. 3:9; 6:19). New creation in him is a relationship founded upon what is not only unseen but also most real. "Now faith is the substance of things hoped for, the evidence of things not seen" (Heb. 11:1, KJV). The mystery of the gospel will seem strange until by the Holy Spirit, it is made to address a person's spiritual hunger. Using memorized proof texts for God's existence or debates about creation will not win postmodern people to Christ. But an authentic story about the transforming work of the Holy Spirit in one's own life and an invitation into the divine mystery can address any deeply felt spiritual hunger.

The celebration of the sacraments for entering the mystery of the gospel should play a significant role in our churches. The very meaning of sacrament is "holy mystery." Something divine and redemptive happens in the sacraments of baptism and the Lord's Supper, something beyond our comprehension. The modern mood wants to explain it all. Instead, we should learn to participate in the sacred wonder of the sacraments and all other means of grace. Inviting non-Christians into the mystery of the sacraments, this sacred space, is an important way of proclaiming the good news of redemption in a postmodern world.

CONCLUSION

Jesus said the fields were ready for harvest (John 4:35). That hasn't changed. Neither has Jesus's appeal for laborers (Matt. 9:38). Therefore, we are still commissioned to "go and make disciples" (28:19, NIV). The harvest fields are ripe with those who have discovered that postmodernity without Christ places them at the lonely center of their world where they become their own "god." The result is a life void of meaning and hope. Witness the accelerating rate of suicides in the United Sates.[12] Suicide is now the second leading cause of death for people ages fifteen to twenty-four.[13] Many people find themselves isolated and dissatisfied with life.

Jesus knew the harvest would always be ready. His appeal was that there would be a sufficient number of laborers. Our postmodern era is in need of laborers who authentically know Jesus Christ and who are ready to invite others into the life of Jesus. May he be made "visible in our bodies" (2 Cor. 4:10, NRSV).

Brianna and I are from different generations. But we enjoy our conversations. She enjoys hearing about my travels and other things I am doing. Stories of compassion and life transformation interest her most. Our relationship will continue, not because I am anxious to make her a convert, but because I love her with the heart of Christ. That's why I share with her the good news I have found in Jesus Christ.

Questions for Consideration

1. In what ways does this chapter make you feel uncomfortable?
2. Instead of opposing postmodernity, how can the church lean into the era and find creative approaches to evangelism?
3. Think about your own spiritual life, and take a few moments to consider your story. What is the good news that you can share?
4. Where is your local harvest field? Where would you be willing to go to take Jesus to those in need?

Additional Resources

Grenz, Stanley J. *A Primer on Postmodernism*. Grand Rapids: Eerdmans, 1996.

Kallenberg, Brad J. *Live to Tell: Evangelism in a Postmodern Age*. Grand Rapids: Brazos Press, 2002.

Kisau, Paul M. "What Postmodernism Means for Evangelism." February 2007. Lausanne World Pulse Archives. http://www.lausanneworldpulse.com/themedarticles-php/624/02-2007.

Newbigin, Lesslie. *The Gospel in a Pluralist Society*. Grand Rapids: Eerdmans, 1989. Kindle.

Nieuwhof, Carey. "Five Important Ways Evangelism Is Shifting in Our Post-Christian World." CareyNieuwhof.com. https://careynieuwhof.com/5-important-ways-evangelism-is-shifting-in-a-post-christian-world/.

Root, Andrew. *Faith Formation in a Secular Age: Responding to the Church's Obsession with Youthfulness*. Ministry in a Secular Age, vol. 1. Grand Rapids: Baker, 2017. Kindle.

3

REPENT AND BELIEVE THE GOOD NEWS

THE GOSPEL AND EVANGELISM

Kent Brower, PhD

At the heart of any Wesleyan approach to evangelism is "the gospel," the good news about Jesus Messiah, Son of God. Mark starts his writing with these words, and Jesus's ministry begins with the announcement that "the time is fulfilled, and the kingdom of God has come near; repent, and believe in the [Gospel]" (1:15, NRSV).

Just what is the gospel? Some might summarize it this way: God, through the cross, has forgiven our sins and prepared us for heaven.[1] And that would be right so far as it goes. But such a "thin, lightweight understanding of salvation and the *missio Dei*"[2] risks distorting both the calling of God's people and diminishing the mission of God. There is far more to a biblical picture of the gospel.

All of us are called to participate in the redemptive mission of God.[3] If understood in this way, we will have an enlarged vision of the gospel and "re-imagine" evangelism as active participation in proclaiming the good news about Jesus Messiah.

THE GOSPEL

The word "gospel" occurs over ninety times in the New Testament, seventy of which are Pauline.[4] Each of the four biographies[5] of Jesus is termed "the gospel according to . . ." This is more than a title, however. "Gospel" is the good news that the whole direction of God's good purposes for his called people and his created order are now being fulfilled and finding their focus in the life, ministry, death, resurrection, and ascension of Jesus Messiah. This story is the fulcrum of God's rescue plan.[6]

The gospel in the New Testament has a long prologue.[7] Isaiah uses cognate terms that focus on announcing the good news.[8] In 40:9, the good news comes from Jerusalem itself to the cities of Judaea. In 52:7, it is the announcement of peace and salvation from God to Jerusalem. In 60:1, it is the proclamation of God's salvation, the redemption of God's people from exile and oppression.[9]

"Gospel" also has a Greco-Roman context. One text lauds the reign of the divine Caesar Augustus whose powerful military brings "salvation" and peace to the world.[10] Luke 2 implicitly contrasts the good news about Jesus the Messiah with the power and authority of Caesar. Jesus, Savior, Messiah, Lord, brings peace on earth (v. 10). This good news is in contrast to the good news imposed by Caesar on a subjugated people. But it is in harmony with the good news in Scripture.[11]

IN THE BEGINNING

Scripture starts with the creator God speaking all things into existence. Creation is good. It culminates in the creation of humankind made in the image and likeness of God. God gives humans a responsibility *in* and *to* creation (Gen. 1:26-30): "a role to play—a mission—from which he never releases us."[12]

The garden-of-Eden story displays the heart of the Creator. It focuses upon the relationships between all created things. Creation is in a symbiotic ecosystem of harmonious relationship. The humans are to reflect the light and love of their Creator to each other. And they are to mediate the love of their Creator in all their connections to the rest of creation. Humans are to live in dynamic harmony with the Creator and the rest of creation.

Genesis pictures the Lord God walking in the garden in the midst of creation—a sacred space made holy by the presence of God. The picture has temple overtones. God empowers humans to care for his creation and to worship by trusting the Creator fully. In this temple-like garden are two trees—the Tree of Life and the Tree of Knowledge of Good and Evil. The Tree of Life is for all—the bounteous provision of the always loving and life-giving Creator. But God takes responsibility for the other tree: he is the judge of good and evil, not Adam and Eve. They would simply need to trust the Creator on this matter.

All goes well until the humans fail to trust their Creator. They trust instead the voice urging independence from God. They no longer honor God as God. Once that primary relationship is marred, all other relationships break down. The man and woman hide from God and from each other. Human solidarity is replaced by distrust; fratricide and genocide litter the pages of Scripture. War becomes, and remains, the most grotesque image of marred human relationships. Instead of loving and faithful companionship, dominance and exploitation poison human relationships. The created order descends into antagonism.

Humans continue to bear the image of their creator, but it is now distorted. Tending the garden becomes work. Humans become parasites in the garden and are driven out; they are no longer able to properly reflect the image of God or worship the creator God in this sacred space. In short, all relationships are damaged beyond human repair.

After the tragic description of human folly, the rest of Scripture is the story of God's rescue plan for his creation, which culminates in the greater garden, the city of God. And it is all about the Messiah.

ISRAEL'S STORY: TO EGYPT AND BACK

God's rescue plan makes its decisive start in the call of Abraham.

This is an epic account of God's provision, mercy, and faithfulness to creation already begun in the covenant with Noah.[13] But the story of Israel itself is one of tragedy, aspects of which are actually part of the mission of God.[14]

God's covenant with Abraham features three things: land, nation, and blessing. As the story unfolds, it becomes clearer that the promise of land and nation has a purpose: so that the nations might be blessed (see Gen. 12:3). This means being rescued from their alienation from the Creator and brought back into that relationship for which they were created in the first place.

The stories of the patriarchs shape Israel's understanding of God and itself. He is the covenant-making God who promises and delivers despite obstacles. Abraham and Sarah are childless, hardly a promising start to a great nation. When at last Sarah does have a son, the confidence of Abraham and that of Isaac in the faithfulness of Yahweh (God's name revealed to Moses [Exod. 3:1-15]) are tried to the extreme. The stories of Rebecca's twins are messy and disturbing, full of deception and dishonesty. By the time the fraught relationships in this dysfunctional family are over, Jacob's children are in Egypt as refugees, dependent upon a brother sold into slavery by his brothers.

After Joseph's death, Abraham's descendants flourish in Egypt. But they are still aliens and slaves. They are increasingly oppressed by the Egyptians: "The Israelites groaned under their slavery, and cried out. . . . God heard their groaning, and God remembered his covenant with Abraham, Isaac, and Jacob" (Exod. 2:23-24, NRSV).

Moses, a child of Levite parents, is brought up in the privilege and power of Pharaoh's household.[15] Under Moses's leadership, Israel is rescued from the Egyptians by the miraculous hand of God. This is Israel's foundation story, forever celebrated at Passover. God shapes the people into a kingdom of priests and a holy nation (19:5-6). God tells them they are to be holy as he is holy (Lev. 19:2). This means they are to reflect the essence of God's love for everyone and participate in his rescue plan for the entire created order. Israel's mission is to "mediate God's life-giving blessings to the nations and, indeed, even to the earth and its non-human inhabitants."[16]

To accomplish this, they must separate themselves from the idolatrous practices of the surrounding nations. In their communal life, Israel must embody who God is.[17] They are "the only visible image of Israel's God to the nations around them."[18]

For Israel, the promised land is both blessing and threat. If they wish to prosper in the land, Deuteronomy makes it clear that they must choose life—God's path of mission to the nations. By doing so, they will participate in the riches of God's blessing. But if they forget their calling in God's mission to the nations, and forget their identity as aliens, they will thereby choose death; the land will spew them out (Lev. 18:24-30).

Three characteristics were supposed to mark Israel. *First*, God hears the cry of the oppressed and acts. God's concern for the marginalized saturates Scripture. The gospel is for them. *Second*, Israel's calling as God's holy people is entirely the gracious action of God, who rescues them and makes them into his holy people. It was never primarily about them but always about God's great rescue plan for his entire created order. No matter how often that calling is obscured, through distortion, disobedience, and failure, the calling and mission to be a kingdom of priests and a holy nation continues. *Third*, even when they possess the land, they are to remember they are perpetual aliens in the land—it belongs to Yahweh. They must always remind themselves of their roots and live in light of that: "You shall not wrong or oppress a resident alien, for you were aliens in the land of Egypt" (Exod. 22:21, NRSV; see also Lev. 19:34; 25:23).

ISRAEL'S STORY: TO EXILE AND BACK

The story from conquest to exile is honest and direct. Israel possesses the land, but there is little rest. The people themselves struggle to maintain their faithfulness to Yahweh as well as their unity. From the period of the judges to Samuel, Yahweh is king. But tension is clear in the move from Samuel to the unfortunate Saul, and the establishment of the Davidic monarchy. Eventually David's reign is consolidated in Jerusalem. The central shrine is relocated there, and despite his covenant-breaking choices leading to disastrous family relationships, David passes into the story as the ideal king. David is a "man after [God's] own heart" (1 Sam. 13:14, NRSV; Acts 13:22).

David's and Solomon's reigns mark the zenith of Israel's power and influence. But disunity, idolatry, treachery, and loss follow.[19] First the Assyrians force the Northern Kingdom into exile in 721 BCE. By 586 BCE, the destruction of Jerusalem and the temple by the Babylonians and the deportation to Babylon leave the promised land under occupation, the nation in tatters, and Yahweh's name profaned instead of honored and worshipped.

During those bleak years, prophetic voices bring encouragement. The exile was never intended to be the end of the story. For the prophets, exile is a time of repentance, purification, and renewal of the people.[20] The prophets announce good news to the exiles. God's purposes remain unshaken; his mission will continue. The righteous remnant will return to Zion, the temple will be rebuilt, the son of David will again rule over God's kingdom, and God will again dwell in their midst.

Some of the people do return. But restoration is neither as glorious nor as complete as they hoped. Still, God might restore them fully, sometime in the future; the cry of the prophet "O that you would tear open the heavens and come down" (Isa. 64:1, NRSV) nicely sums up the longing. God could do a new thing. He could gather the scattered from the four winds and raise up a son of David who would be the anointed one (Messiah) of God.

Hope persists, with several false dawns along the way. Judah again enjoys a quasi-independent status for about a century. But by the end of this period, it is clear that the Hasmonean dynasty is not the fulfillment of the prophetic hopes. And so, the people, although in possession of the land, and with ethnic purity now the determining factor in identity, still are psychologically and spiritually longing for something more—a new exodus, a new presence of God in the midst of his people, who would once again be on God's mission.

Indeed, God's promises would be met. But not quite in the way most of them expected—and not yet. They are still in exile.[21]

THE GOOD NEWS: UNTO US A CHILD IS BORN

The Gospel writers are unanimous: God's new thing is happening. That's the message of John the Baptist who appears as a voice crying in the wilderness. Messiah is coming, prepare his way, repent, and believe. The kingdom of God is arriving.

The birth narratives set the scene. Matthew starts with Jesus's genealogy, beginning from Abraham. His point is clear: this is the one on whom the promise to Abraham with its blessing of all nations will rest. Joseph names him and thereby announces that he will save his people from their sins. The child, conceived in Mary from the Holy Spirit, will be called Emmanuel, "God is with us" (1:21-23, NRSV). This is extraordinary: Jesus, child of Abraham, Savior of his people, is God with us.

The importance of this child's birth is signaled by the arrival of magi. Matthew sees this as another scriptural motif: Gentiles are paying homage to the Bethlehem-born son of David. In a warning against the murderous paranoia of the Roman puppet King Herod, who is not the rightful son of David, the messenger of the Lord instructs the holy family to become refugees in Egypt. For Matthew, Jesus is the embodiment of Israel.[22]

At his baptism, Jesus fully identifies with Israel, embracing the mission of God. The voice from heaven confirms the astonishing claim that this human on whom the Spirit rests is "my beloved son" (3:17, author's translation; Mark 1:11). For Matthew, the birth of Jesus gathers up Israel's story to this point. God is again among his people to lead them on the rescue mission in fulfilment of the covenant with Abraham.

Luke's birth story is similar but not identical. Here, too, Jesus's lineage is set out. But Luke's list extends back to Jesus as "son of Adam, son of God" (3:38, NRSV). When combined with the annunciation (1:26-38), Luke pictures Jesus's birth as a new beginning for humanity. Mary will name him Jesus, he "will be called the Son of the Most High," and he will reign on the throne of his ancestor David forever (vv. 32-33, NRSV). Jesus embodies the purposes of God's call of Israel. In Jesus, God is fulfilling all "the promise he made to our ancestors, to Abraham and to his descendants forever" (v. 55, NRSV).

Luke gives attention to the Baptist's role as well. John prepares the way for the Lord (v. 76). He calls Israel to return to its calling as God's people (v. 17). Jesus is the one for whose coming the holy remnant has been praying. Zechariah confirms the belief that in Jesus, God "has raised up a mighty savior for us in the house of his servant David" (v. 69, NRSV) in God's covenant faithfulness (vv. 72-73). The aged Simeon grasps the breadth of the mission of the "Lord's Messiah" (2:26, NRSV): he will be "a light for revelation to the Gentiles and for glory to your people Israel" (v. 32, NRSV).

John's[23] Gospel has the most explicit description of Jesus's divine identity (1:1-4). He is the Word made flesh, who dwelt in the midst of his people (v. 14). He, not the temple, is the locus of God's holy presence (2:21). He is the "Holy One of God" (6:69, NRSV). Jesus's identity is known from the start.[24] His identity is inextricably bound to God's mission: it is out of the Father's love for the world that the Son is sent (3:16).

For all four Evangelists, the coming of Jesus is the good news because in Jesus's arrival, Moses and the prophets find their fulfillment. Isaiah's new thing has arrived. Israel's King, the Messiah, the Savior of the world, the good news, the bringer of the peace of God to his broken and bloodied people, is here.

THE GOOD NEWS: THE MISSION RENEWED

After his baptism and temptation, and John's imprisonment,[25] Jesus comes announcing the good news: "The time is fulfilled, and the kingdom of God [is already arriving];[26] repent, and believe in the good news" (Mark 1:14-15, NRSV and author's translation).

The calling of disciples is the first act: this is the mission of the people of God. After the call of the four, Jesus's identity is announced by the unclean spirit in the synagogue. He is the "Holy One of God" (v. 24, NRSV), gathering around him a disparate group of people. God's saving presence is experienced: the marginalized are welcomed, the unclean are cleansed, the sick are healed, and demons are exorcised.

This ministry leads to the calling of the Twelve. Curiously, the Twelve are not significant as individuals. They are important, however, as a group because of what they represent. In a clear echo of God's call of Moses and the elders, Jesus calls his disciples to the mountain where Jesus (re)creates the (re)new(ed) people of God. They are "to be with him, and to be sent out to proclaim the message, and to have authority to cast out demons" (vv. 14-15, NRSV). These apostles participate in the mission of God. They are to feed the hungry, exorcise demons, heal the sick, and welcome the outcast. And they do precisely that (see 6:7-13, 30). According to Luke, they have a role in "judging the twelve tribes of Israel" (22:30, NRSV). Significantly, after the death of Judas Iscariot, his place in the Twelve is filled (Acts 1:15-28). They are, thus, the representatives of all Israel, the gathered people of God.

They are not alone, however. Jesus continues to gather around him people for the mission. In this call, blood ties do not matter. All that matters is being with the Holy One of God and participating in God's mission.[27] In fact, Jesus's invitation is wide open. Once the disciples actually figure out who Jesus is—"You are the Messiah" (Mark 8:29, NRSV)—he calls the crowd along with the Twelve and says, "Whoever wants to be my disciple must deny themselves and take up their cross daily and follow me" (Luke 9:23, NIV).

The mission of God is costly. In all of the Gospels, opposition comes from the religious and political establishment, as well as from the spirit world. Jesus explains the cost of discipleship on the journey to Jerusalem, but the disciples continue to struggle with it. They follow Jesus into Jerusalem, probably hoping that Jesus would establish his throne and that they would begin ruling alongside him (see Mark 10:35-40).

Far more significant for Jesus is the Passover meal, which points back to the gathering and shaping of the covenant people at Sinai as "a kingdom of priests and a holy nation" (Exod. 19:1-6, NIV).[28] Now Jesus retells the Passover meal in a way that culminates in (re)forming the Twelve into the vanguard of this (re)new(ed) covenant community. In a prophetic act, he breaks the bread and pours out the wine. He announces that this is [*his*] blood of the new covenant (see Matt. 26:28; Luke 22:20). At this table, which proclaims the good news (see 1 Cor. 11:26), Jesus's disciples anticipate their participation in Jesus's suffering, death, and resurrection. In a profound sense, they themselves *become* the gospel through their participation.

Ultimately, the authorities condemn Jesus to his cross. But the authorities themselves symbolize and evidence human brokenness. Jesus embraces the human condition fully. He dies so that God's rescue plan for the entire created order can be fulfilled. The disciples fail to stand by Jesus, but Jesus gathers them as scattered sheep and leads them into Galilee (Matt. 28:16-18).[29]

In Matthew, Jesus first sends his followers "to the lost sheep of the house of Israel. As you go, proclaim the good news, 'The kingdom of heaven [is arriving]'" (10:6-7, NRSV and author's translation). But to understand this as an exclusive calling misses Matthew's point: these are they who have lost their way, are still in exile, and have forgotten their mission. Matthew's concern is that a renewed Israel, responding to the good news, might again embrace its missional calling from God. Jesus embodies that mission because he is the fulfillment of all the Law and the Prophets.

Matthew concludes his Gospel with the Great Commission. Now the gospel is to be proclaimed to the nations, who, in turn, are invited to be transformed into part of God's holy people. They, too, are to join in the redemptive mission of God. Jesus remains with them—the divine presence in the divine mission: "And remember, I am with you always, to the end of the age" (28:20, NRSV).[30]

THE GOOD NEWS: THE NAZARETH MANIFESTO

Jesus, filled with the Spirit, returns from the wilderness to Galilee. Word is spreading, and Jesus is teaching in the synagogues. He comes to Nazareth and, as was his practice, goes to synagogue on Sabbath. He reads from Isaiah 61:1-2, perhaps the appointed synagogue *haftorah* reading (a reading from the Prophets after reading from the Torah) for the day. To this point, the story is unexceptional. But once Jesus finishes the reading, "he began to say to them, 'Today this scripture has been fulfilled in your hearing'" (Luke 4:21, NRSV).

For Luke, this statement from Isaiah is programmatic, predictive. "The Spirit of the Lord is upon me," Jesus says, "because he has anointed me to bring good news to the poor. He has sent me to proclaim release to the captives and recovery of sight to the blind, to let the oppressed go free, to proclaim the year of the Lord's favor" (vv. 18-19, NRSV).[31]

Good news to the poor, forgiveness of debt, and release from slavery cannot be confined to the spiritual. Isaiah 61:1-2 is conceptually linked to the year of Jubilee (Lev. 25:8-13), especially with the line "to proclaim the year of the Lord's favor" (Luke 4:19, NRSV; Isa. 61:2). And Jubilee has unmistakable economic overtones.[32] Thus to hear this good news to the poor in a restricted, internal sense is to mishear it.

But Jesus's words spoken in the synagogue (Luke 4:16-30) are more than a Jubilee theme. They are also an invitation, a message of forgiveness and release. Jesus's hearers might well have in mind the end of Roman occupation and the accompanying sense of continuing exile. But there is more. They are free to become who they are called to be: the people of God on the mission of God for the world. Jesus is inviting them to repent and return to God's purposes for them as a blessing to the nations.

Two further points are important. *First*, Jesus stops his Isaiah reading before Isaiah 61:2 announces "the day of vengeance of our God" (NRSV).[33] The theme of judgment does occur in Luke; this is the time of rescue, of transformation, of salvation. *Second*, the response of the hearers is, at first, astonishment at Jesus's audacious claim. But when he pointedly illustrates the gracious activity of God by reference to a Sidonian woman and a Syrian military commander, the listeners are outraged.[34] This good news, they think, should be only for them, not for outsiders. In their assessment, they completely miss the breadth and the purpose of the new day that Jesus is inaugurating (Luke 4:25-30).

Luke gives particular attention to Jesus's welcome of all people to the table, including tax collectors and sinners. This troubles the Pharisees because they understand holiness as essentially separation from impurity. Holiness and purity are indeed linked, but "time and again the compassion of Jesus for those who are the marginalized overrides the legitimate concern for purity."[35]

Jesus also dines with Pharisees. On one memorable occasion he gives a lesson on love and forgiveness to Simon the Pharisee (7:36-50). When the Pharisees complain that Jesus is compromising his purity by his indiscriminate table companions, he invites them to join the celebration rather than sit on the sidelines offering self-righteous judgment.

The collection of parables in Luke 15 makes the point clearly.[36] The stories of the lost sheep and the lost coin show that "God is the persistent, seeking, gracious and loving God who extravagantly celebrates the rescue of every single repentant sinner."[37] The third parable is even more profound. Here the lost son is embraced even before he asks forgiveness. "For the father, the only important thing is that 'my son was dead, and is alive again; he was lost, and is found' (15:24 [KJV])."[38] Sadly, the elder brother, who has been faithful rather than faithless, is angry about the welcome given to his feckless brother. So he stays away from the celebration. "But this father loves his elder son with the same unquenchable love, and so goes out to find him. Celebration of the restored relationship is essential, but that celebration should include the elder brother."[39] The righteous are not excluded. Rather, their understanding of holiness, purity, and mission needs revision.

Even the rich have a place in the people of God. But their participation is contingent upon their attitude and behavior toward the poor, the marginalized, and sinners. If they are not generous in their hospitality and welcoming, they will themselves become the outsiders and exclude themselves from the banquet.[40]

THE GOOD NEWS: ABIDE AND GO[41]

Throughout the whole story to this point, the mission has been based upon who God *is*. In John, God is love (see 1 John 4:8, 16) and triune, existing in an "unceasing movement of mutual love."[42] The *missio Dei*, the mission of God, is not something external to God. Rather, love is at the heart of it (see John 3:16).

God's work is Jesus's work. Gorman notes, "To be sent as Jesus was sent is to be in a relationship of mutual indwelling with the Sender such that the works one does are the works of the indwelling one. For Jesus, there was an ontological unity with the Father. . . . It was impossible for him not to do the works of God. . . . Nonetheless, being fully human, Jesus needed to *willingly* do his Father's will."[43]

But what about Jesus's followers? In the astonishing language of John 17, the disciples—and later readers of the gospel—are invited into a mutual indwelling with Father and Son, and with each other.[44] This does not mean believers are absorbed into the Divine. Rather, they are invited into the circle of divine love.

This mutual indwelling has implications.[45]

First, it expects the followers of Jesus to be a hospitable community of mutual participation with each other in the same way the Holy Trinity is being in community. This is why Jesus offers a new command: "that you love one another" (John 13:34, NRSV). Such a community has forgiveness, repentance, restoration, and transformation at its heart. It comes from the gracious welcome into the divine hospitality and is worked out in the flesh-and-blood community of people.

The *second* implication is participation in the being and mission of God. The mission of God—the works of the Father in the Gospel of John—is to be continued by Jesus's followers.

> As Jesus did the works of His Father (5:17, 19-21, 30), so we will also do these works, including belief in the One who sent the Son (6:28-29). Indeed, the works that we will do will be greater than those Jesus himself has done because He is going to the Father and the Spirit will be upon all (14:11-12). These works are part of the big purposes of God, part of the mission of God in the created order.[46]

It is precisely as the Father has sent the Son that the disciples are sent. The resurrected Jesus says to the assembled apostles "As the Father has sent me, so I send you," infuses them with the Holy Spirit, and summarizes the mission: "If you forgive the sins of any, they are forgiven them; if you retain the sins of any, they are retained" (20:21-23, NRSV). The disciples "are to exercise the prerogatives of God in carrying out this mission . . . [of] forgiveness of sins in 20:23."[47] At the same time, "Forgiveness is ultimately *God's* work, not that of the disciples, who are certainly agents but *only* agents."[48]

For the disciples to participate in God's mission entails both witnessing to Jesus and his presence with them and doing the works the Father has given the Son to do. The disciples love one another (13:34; 15:12, 17) as a witness to their participation in the life of the triune God. This love is possible only through the presence of the Spirit and through participation in the hospitality of the Holy Trinity.[49]

Jesus prays for his followers: "As you have sent me into the world, so I have sent them into the world. And for their sakes I sanctify myself, so that they also may be sanctified in truth" (17:18-19, NRSV). This is a prayer for mission for the holy people of God engaged in the mission of God.

"MY GOSPEL" (ACCORDING TO PAUL): THE CLIMAX OF THE STORY[50]

The apostle Paul refers to the "gospel" more than any other New Testament writer. He himself is set apart for the gospel, which is all about Jesus, Son of David and Son of God. It is the good news of God's salvation for everyone, to Jews and then to Gentiles. For Paul, this is "a new reality which builds upon and includes the old, bringing it to its intended purpose."[51]

Philippians 2:1-12 offers an outline of the gospel.[52] The fully divine Messiah Jesus is seen in his embracing the mission of God. Jesus simultaneously is the fully obedient Son and participant in the human condition of alienation by enduring a humiliating death.[53] Jesus's faithful obedience to the Father, unlike that of Adam and Israel, is the means through which the faithfulness of God to his redemptive promises is actualized.[54] The result is that Jesus is highly exalted and the good purposes of God are accomplished in the perfectly obedient incarnate Son, all leading to the ultimate glory of God.

Paul uses this summary as a model for the lives of believers. "Let this mind be in you" (v. 5, KJV), he writes, so that you "might work out your own salvation because it is God who is at work in you for his purposes" (vv. 12-13, author's paraphrase). The central part of 2:1-13, verses 6-11, summarizes incarnational theology. But if they are read in isolation from the whole passage, we risk reducing the gospel to a formal "belief" in Jesus.

"MY GOSPEL": PARTICIPATION "IN CHRIST"

Paul wants his readers "not merely to *believe* the gospel but to *become* the gospel, and in so doing to participate in the very life and mission of God."[55]

"Participation" is a strong word for Paul. Believers are "in Christ" by entering into his death and resurrection. To participate in Christ is to become part of the people of God; it involves being transformed into the image of God's Son and enabled through the presence of the indwelling Spirit to join in the mission of God. The people of God participate in the faithfulness of the Messiah, the *koinonia* of Christ's sufferings, and share in the mission of God.[56]

Participation in Christ is transformational: "So if anyone is in Christ, there is a new creation" (2 Cor. 5:17, NRSV). This is intensely personal but never simply individual. "The holy people of God is more than a collective for which one has a personal membership card. People who are incorporated into the new creation in Christ, the new solidarity in Christ, are also new creatures in Christ."[57] This is a real and present reality.[58]

Those who are in Christ are renewed in the image of the Creator (see Col. 3:10-17), the new starting point in the relationship with the Creator. It is that "inner dynamic of the Spirit which has begun the process of restoring the *imago dei* [the image of God], marred by Adam's sin."[59] Of course, the fullness of new creation still awaits the resurrection of the body (Rom. 8:11, 23). Christians still live in fallen flesh and broken societies, facing forces largely hostile to God.[60]

God's holy people are all those who participate in the Messiah. Identification of God's holy people is no longer connected to "national identity, nor any other secondary distinction. God's new creation is solely through participation in Christ. In him God is creating a new people to be agents of his reconciling purposes."[61] This is fundamental to Paul's argument: the children of Abraham, those who are to be a blessing to the nations, are not determined by genetics. No human barriers exist.[62] Those in Christ are part of a new people of God—*now*—and are done with old prejudices born of the distorted standards of this present age.[63]

"MY GOSPEL": AGENTS OF RECONCILIATION

The gospel is intensely missional. It is good news to be shared and embodied. Crucially, those who are saved are rescued not only for their own sake but also to become agents of reconciliation (2 Cor. 5:18-20).[64]

Believers are to be the center from which God's mission to the world proceeds because they are the temple of God. When his Corinthian readers are faced with divisions, Paul asks, "Do you not know that you [together] are God's temple and that God's Spirit dwells in you? If anyone destroys God's temple, God will destroy that person. For God's temple is holy, and you are that temple" (1 Cor. 3:16-17, NRSV).

This is crucial. No longer is the presence of God thought to be confined to a static physical temple. Rather, those in the Messiah in whom the Spirit dwells, the holy people of God, are, *collectively*, the walking temple of God. But this is also *personal*. What Christians do with their bodies matters: "Do you not know that your body is a temple of the Holy Spirit within you, which you have from God, and that you are not your own?" (6:19, NRSV).

Renewal in God's image entails restoration of damaged relationships. If love permeates relationships within the people of God, they live as

God's chosen and holy ones (see Col. 3:12) and "fulfill the law of Christ" (Gal. 5:14; 6:2, NRSV). They become models of God's purposes for all human relationships. To be sure, many times the church falls short of that demonstration; just listen to Paul's letter to the Corinthians. But the church's failures don't diminish our being called to serve God's purpose, his plan of reconciliation now being worked out in and through the people of God.

But the gospel as preached by Paul is even greater than that.[65] The gospel is God's rescue plan for the entire created order. This involves restoring a right relationship with God, other humans, and the rest of creation (Rom. 8:18-25). Nothing short of this comprehensive understanding of the significance of the cross and Jesus's resurrection does justice to Paul's vision of the gospel.

The implications of this are immense as they relate to proclaiming the gospel. "If the salvation offered in Christ is as universal in scope as Paul believes it to be, then God's big purposes must also include restoring the entire created order to its intended purpose."[66] It follows that "God's holy people see creation through different eyes. As people renewed in the image of the loving, creating, sustaining and redeeming God, our stewardship of his world is to be carried out in the context of love and harmony, not exploitation and abuse. The saints care about the planet."[67]

THE HOLY GOD WITH THE HOLY PEOPLE IN THE HOLY PLACE

The gospel, the good news of God's rescue plan, is ongoing. The kingdom of God is here, but not yet in its fullness. Sometimes the "not yet" can seem overwhelming. The people of God are embattled. The Roman Empire, with its vast military machine, its boastful leaders, its overwhelming enforced peace, and its colossal wealth concentrated in the hands of a few, could have tempted the early church to succumb to Rome's blandishments. Then the church would have just become one more part of "empire." Paul and John[68] remind us of our true citizenship (Phil. 3:17-21; John 15:18-27).

So what do the people of God do in such circumstances?

The book of Revelation is written in just such circumstances. As Flemming notes, the question facing the churches in the face of empire is this: "Will they be Christian assemblies who comfortably cohabit with the idolatrous world around them, or will they live in light of God's final purpose for his people?"[69]

In the face of devastation, persecution, and temptation, the seer in Revelation is invited to open his eyes and see the big picture. God is in control, not Caesar. The power of the empire is a mere parody of the power of the slaughtered Lamb. The glitter of the empire is pathetic compared to that which surrounds the throne and the Lamb. The people of God are warned about complacency and compromise.[70] "Resisting captivity to fallen Babylon means that the saints must challenge the ungodly cultural and political ideologies that dominate their world. But they will do so at a cost."[71] Still, "Revelation's answer for the church is not to retreat into a cocoon of pious irrelevance, but to resist Rome's dominant ideology through its prophetic witness (*martyrs*)."[72] Faithful witness is the continuing challenge presented to the church as it participates in the mission of God. Like the first readers of Revelation, our temptation to compromise or become complacent is a real danger.

But if the people of God see the big picture, the courage to be a faithful witness will be born. The big picture as offered in Revelation 21–22 is magnificent. Here "the home of God is among mortals. He will dwell with them; they will be his peoples, and God himself will be with them" (21:3, NRSV). This vision of the city of God is beyond comprehension. But two things are clear. "In this city, boundaries between the sacred and the secular dissolve,"[73] and it is "the final reversal of the story of human sin that separated human beings from the holy presence of God."[74] This is the direction our proclamation of the gospel is taking.

As Christians today, we might also be tempted to despair. But here the words of Hebrews offer encouragement. "As it is, we do not yet see everything in subjection to [him], but we do see Jesus" (Heb. 2:8-9, NRSV and author's translation). So we look "to Jesus the pioneer and perfecter of our faith" (12:2, NRSV) and rest our faith in the sure and certain hope of the resurrection (Rom. 6:4-5; 8:11; Heb. 6:18-19; 1 John 3:2-3).

Questions for Consideration

1. How has this chapter expanded your understanding of the gospel of Jesus Christ?
2. What is the "good news" we Christians are called to declare?
3. What is the mission of God, and what is our role in it?

Additional Resources

Flemming, Dean. *Recovering the Full Mission of God: A Biblical Perspective on Being, Doing and Telling*. Downers Grove, IL: IVP Academic, 2013.

Wright, N. T. *The Challenge of Jesus: Rediscovering Who Jesus Was and Is*. Downers Grove, IL: InterVarsity Press, 1999.

———. *The Day the Revolution Began: Reconsidering the Meaning of Jesus's Crucifixion*. New York: HarperOne, 2016.

4

FOR WHOM IS THE GOSPEL INTENDED?

THE MEANING OF GRACE AND THE GOSPEL'S UNIVERSALITY

Christi Bennett, PhD

THE QUESTION

Glennie's eyelids fluttered open. She surveyed her surroundings—white sheets, white walls, white sink in the corner. A nurse by profession, it did not take Glennie long to recognize her surroundings: hospital! So, then, even the grim reaper didn't want her.

Sexually abused as a child, Glennie had turned to addictions to soothe her pain—anything to dull the ache in her heart. But the pain remained—unrelenting. Her addictions and anger landed Glennie in jail and got her ejected from her brother's house. If anyone needed the saving grace of God, Glennie did. But was God's grace sufficient for a mess like her? Even if it was, she doubted she was on God's preferred list.

Does God have a list? Does God want to redeem some people, but not others? Are some people, by design, outside the reach of God's saving grace? And why do some respond to the invitation of the gospel, but not others?

BIBLICAL BACKGROUND

These questions echo from the pages of Scripture. Who does God love and seek to redeem?

As they languished in slavery in Egypt, the Hebrew people cried out to God for relief (Exod. 2:23). But after God sent Moses back from the wilderness in answer to their prayers, every setback on their road to deliverance made them doubt both Moses and God. Was Yahweh strong enough to overcome the power of Pharaoh? And if he was, why would he bother with a ragtag group of slaves like them?[1]

Later, after they had settled in their land of promise, many Israelites began to believe God cared for them, but not for other people. They thought of Yahweh as their own local god, uninterested in the well-being of others. Consider the prophet Jonah. Even after a terrifying storm, a near-drowning, and a rescue by a great fish, Jonah remained unconvinced that Yahweh should show concern for the Ninevites to whom God had sent him (Jon. 3:10–4:11).

Much later, even after the day of Pentecost, it took the vision of a menagerie of unclean animals on a sheet to convince the apostle Peter the gospel should be proclaimed to Gentiles (Acts 10:9-18).

Beginning in the first chapter of Genesis, the Scriptures announce there is only one true God over all creation.[2] In Exodus 19:5 we hear God say, "The whole earth is mine" (NIV). Psalm 97 sings, "The LORD reigns, let the earth be glad; let the distant shores rejoice" (NIV).[3] The servant songs of Isaiah echo the tune: "It is too small a thing for you to be my servant to restore the tribes of Jacob and bring back those of Israel I have kept. I will also make you a light for the Gentiles, that my salvation may reach to the ends of the earth" (Isa. 49:6, NIV).[4] The prophet Habakkuk anticipated a day when "the earth will be filled with the knowledge of the glory of the LORD as the waters cover the sea" (Hab. 2:14, NIV).

However, a tension exists in the Bible between the *universal*, God as the god over all, and the *particular*, God focused on a specific, elect, called-out people. When we widen our lens on Exodus 19, we hear God say, "Out of all nations you will be my treasured possession. Although the whole earth is mine [universal], you will be for me a kingdom of priests and a holy nation [particular]" (vv. 5-6, NIV). In Genesis 12, God calls Abram and assures him, "I will bless you [particular]" (v. 2, NIV). At the same time God promises, "All peoples on earth will be blessed through you [universal]" (v. 3, NIV).

In the New Testament the apostle Paul tells Timothy that God "wants all people to be saved and to come to a knowledge of the truth" (1 Tim. 2:4, NIV). He tells Titus, "For the grace of God has appeared that offers salvation to all people" (Titus 2:11, NIV). To the Romans Paul declares, "Consequently, just as one trespass resulted in condemnation for all people, so also one righteous act resulted in justification and life for all people" (Rom. 5:18, NIV). And to the Corinthian Christians, Paul proclaims, Christ "died for all" (2 Cor. 5:15, NIV). Finally, the gospel of Jesus Christ that delivers believers from the kingdom of darkness and transfers them to the "kingdom of [God's] beloved Son" (Col. 1:13, RSV), Paul tells the Colossians, is being proclaimed to "every creature under heaven" (v. 23, RSV).[5]

But this same Paul told the Romans, "For those [God] foreknew he also predestined to be conformed to the image of his Son" (Rom. 8:29, RSV). To the Ephesians Paul wrote, "[God] predestined us for adoption to sonship through Jesus Christ, in accordance with his pleasure and will" (Eph. 1:5, NIV).

So on the one hand, Paul declares a Christ who died for all (3:8-9). On the other hand, he seems to indicate that God has chosen, predestined, elected only some people for "adoption to sonship" (1:5-7, NIV).

So we ask, Who are the *all* for whom Christ died? Is the *all universal*, meant for all persons? Or is God's grace meant for and directed toward a predestined *few*?

THE FAVOR OF AN INVITATION

I knew they were getting married. The groom's parents were my friends and informed me of the plans. I watched the mail for the fancy envelope that would contain a wedding invitation. But—it never came. The wedding venue the bride and groom chose was small. The bride, whom I had never met, had charge of the guest list. I lived hundreds of miles from the wedding site. Perhaps I should have been unsurprised not to "make the cut." Maybe I was out of favor with the bride, or at least not "in her favor." Whatever the reason, I was not "graced" with an invitation.

Christians often speak of grace as God's unmerited favor. The angel encouraged Mary with the words, "Do not be afraid, Mary; you have found favor with God" (Luke 1:30, NIV). The Greek word used for favor is *charis*. It is translated "grace" in Ephesians 2:8-9: "For it is by *grace* you have been saved, through faith—and this is not from yourselves, it is the gift of God—not by works, so that no one can boast" (NIV, emphasis added). As we consider the biblical tension between the universal and the particular, we are actually asking, Who receives God's favor? Who is invited to receive God's salvation? Is the invitation limited? How far does God's saving grace extend?

Jesus, through whom we know God most fully, had a way of surprising the Jewish leaders with his answers to these questions. The Pharisees had a list of people whom they would never favor with a greeting, much less offer an invitation: tax collectors, sinners, Samaritans, and Gentiles, for starters. Jesus kept reaching outside that list. He invited Matthew (Levi), a tax collector, to be his disciple (Matt. 9:9; Mark 2:13-14). He invited another tax collector, Zacchaeus, to host him for dinner (Luke 19:1-10). Jesus offered living water to a Samaritan woman (John 4:1-26). He commended the sinful woman who anointed his feet (Luke 7:36-50). He healed the daughter of a Gentile (Matt. 15:21-28). "I have not come to call the righteous," Jesus declared, "but sinners to repentance" (Luke 5:32, NIV). He told parables about lost sheep and lost sons (Luke 15), parables intended to declare his favor toward those who had long been out of favor.

Before he ascended to heaven, Jesus commanded his disciples to "go and make disciples of all nations" (Matt. 28:19, NIV). They assumed at first that Jesus meant, "Make disciples of Jews from all nations." But when God poured out his Spirit on Cornelius and his household (Acts 10:44-47; 11:15-17; 15:7-9), Jesus's disciples discovered that God also intends to favor (grace) Gentiles with forgiveness of sins.

If then, God does have a list, it must include tax collectors, sinners, Samaritans, women, Jews, and Gentiles. Never in the Gospels does Jesus reject anyone who seeks him. If Jesus had a list, it included everyone, including his enemies (Matt. 5:43-45; Luke 23:34). As Peter declared to the household of Cornelius, "I now realize how true it is that God does not show favoritism but accepts from every nation the one who fears him and does what is right" (Acts 10:34, NIV).

Glennie's inclusion in God's grace, his favor, surprised even her. Yet God did include her. God began by sending a compassionate Christian to live in the mobile home next to hers. The neighbor noticed Glennie's distress. She asked her pastor's wife to help her minister to Glennie. The pastor's wife visited Glennie in the hospital and stood with her in her battle against addiction. Glennie was surprised by God's grace being extended to her through these godly people.

A LIMITED GUEST LIST?

Does God have a list that offers saving grace to some while denying it to others? Some Christian leaders have thought so.

Augustine of Hippo (AD 354–430) thought so. He was surprised to find himself in God's favor. Raised by a Christian mother, Augustine knew the way of Christ. But as a young man, he chose destructive paths. He gave free reign to his lusts and vanities. A bright student, Augustine scorned Christianity as intellectually inferior. Instead, he dabbled in various non-Christian religions and philosophies. He became bound by sin. But by the work of God's Holy Spirit, Augustine at last trusted in Christ. Knowing well that God's grace alone had brought him to faith, Augustine argued against a monk named Pelagius. Pelagius taught that humans could, by exercising their own free will, follow Christ and live free of sin. Against Pelagius, Augustine argued that God has a list. God has chosen to save a select number of people. By grace, God moves his elect to faith in Christ.[6] Augustine left no doubt what he believed. "Faith, then, as well in its beginning as in its completion, is God's gift; . . . this gift is given to some, while to some it is not given. . . . But why He delivers one rather than another—'*His judgments are unsearchable, and His ways past finding out.*'"[7]

More than a thousand years later, John Calvin (1509-64), in his *Institutes of the Christian Religion* (1559), adopted Augustine's position. God,

Calvin taught, "once established by his eternal and unchangeable plan those whom he long before determined once for all to receive into salvation, and those whom, on the other hand, he would devote to destruction. . . . This plan was founded upon his freely given mercy, without regard to human worth."[8] This foreordination, election, or predestination God decides in his "secret counsel." God seals the elect (chosen for salvation) by "call and justification," while he shuts off the reprobate (chosen for eternal death) "from knowledge of his name or from sanctification of his Spirit."[9]

Calvin's followers came to be known as the "Reformed" branch of Protestantism. In the seventeenth century, Reformed theologians in the Netherlands (at the Synod of Dort, 1619) and England (at the Westminster Assembly, 1646) hardened their teachings about predestination. They taught that (1) sin has so extensively depraved human nature that humans are utterly unable to respond in faith to God; (2) God's saving grace is unconditional—given to the elect without any preconditions; (3) Christ died only for the elect (those God chose, in his eternal decrees, without reference to their merit, to predestine to eternal life); (4) God's grace works irresistibly to create faith in the elect; and (5) the elect cannot resist or fall away from God's grace.[10] Each point in this system was connected by tight logic. Each point asserted the absolute sovereignty and limited grace of God. When compared with the great mass of those condemned, the elect were few. Salvation of the elect came solely because God (as sovereign monarch) decreed it should be—sovereignly and irresistibly.

When one considers this teaching through the analogy of an invitation, things become strange. If grace is unconditional and irresistible as Augustine and Calvin believed, there can be no genuine "invitation." A wedding invitation comes with the responsibility to accept or reject it. Many invitations include a card for a guest to register her response: "I __will __will not attend." The Scriptures are full of invitations: "Come, follow me" (Matt. 4:19, NIV); "Come to me, all you who are weary and burdened" (11:28, NIV); "Come and see" (John 1:39, KJV); "Let anyone who is thirsty come to me and drink" (7:37, NIV). These invitations summon a response—accept or reject. With the doctrine of irresistible grace, there is no response card, no option; the invitation automatically and irresistibly transports the guest to the wedding.

AN OPEN INVITATION

The early church fathers framed the gospel differently than did Augustine and Calvin. They found in the Bible an open invitation to salvation. Christ died for all and then graciously invited all to receive the gift of redemption. By uniting human nature to himself in the incarnation, and through death on the cross, Jesus made freedom from the powers of darkness possible for all (Col. 2:13-15).[11] As Irenaeus wrote in *Against Heresies*, "as in Adam we do all die, as being of an animal nature, in Christ we may all live, as being spiritual, not laying aside God's handiwork, but the lusts of the flesh, and receiving the Holy Spirit."[12]

Jerome (ca. AD 347–420), translator of the Latin Vulgate Bible, decried the suggestion that there are "some sins which Christ cannot cleanse and sinners for whom Christ did not die."[13] He asked, "What else is this but to say that Christ died in vain? He has indeed died in vain if there are any whom he cannot make alive."[14] John Chrysostom (ca. AD 349–407) preached, "God never compels anyone by necessity and force, but he wills that all be saved, yet he does not force anyone."[15] Theodore of Mopsuestia (ca. AD 350–ca. AD 428) insisted, "The purpose established by God is not that someone may be damned, but that all may be saved . . . indeed his grace is offered to all who want it."[16] They agreed that Christ died to save all and that God extends his invitation to all. All those invited need only to turn and accept God's favor, his grace.

In the second and third centuries the church confronted the Gnostic heresy, an intricate complex of myths, some of which tried to turn Christ into a Gnostic "savior." The Gnostics taught that only special "spiritual" people could be saved. But ordinary "material" people, hopelessly plagued by the "material," could never be saved.[17] Such elitist ideas were antithetical to Christian teaching, which proclaimed that Christ died for all (2 Cor. 5:14) and that "God does not show favoritism" (Acts 10:34; Rom. 2:11; Gal. 2:6, NIV). Early church fathers such as Irenaeus fought against Gnostic elitism.

Like these early church fathers, John Wesley (1703-91) taught that God extends the benefits of Christ's sacrifice to all people. Wesley argued that the Calvinist doctrine of predestination misrepresents God's character: "This is the blasphemy clearly contained in the horrible decree of predestination! And here I fix my foot. On this I join issue with every asserter of it. You represent God as worse than the devil; more false, more cruel, more unjust."[18]

For Wesley, God's sovereignty is a loving, parental sovereignty.[19] He rejected the notion that God "who so loved the world"—this God revealed to us in Jesus Christ—would, by some "secret" counsel, consign many humans to damnation. No, the God we see revealed in John 3:16-17 is a God who gave his only begotten Son to provide every prodigal with a way back to the Father's forgiveness. Further, Wesley objected that the teaching of unconditional election and irresistible grace weakens Christian motivation to pursue holiness and to evangelize those who have not yet heard the gospel.[20] Such a notion of predestination, Wesley insisted, could not have come from God.

Wesley knew that because of sin, human nature has become distorted. It possesses not even a spark of goodness by which to respond to God's offer of grace. But Wesley taught that our merciful God has left none hopeless before him or to their own devices for achieving salvation (Eph. 2:14-18). Jesus, God's only begotten Son, gave his life as an atonement, as a way of reconciliation, for all persons. Through the Holy Spirit, everyone receives an open invitation to enter fellowship with God. "Where sin increased, grace increased all the more" (Rom. 5:20, NIV), or as the gospel of John declares, "Out of his fullness we have all received grace in place of grace already given" (John 1:16, NIV).

Because Christ died for the salvation of all persons, through the Holy Spirit God's prevenient grace (see chap. 5) operates in everyone. God, by this grace and through his Holy Spirit, convicts the world of sin (John 16:7-11), "offers salvation to all people" (Titus 2:11, NIV), and draws them to Christ (John 6:44; 12:32). The Holy Spirit enables everyone who will to respond in obedient faith to God's offer of salvation.[21] Thus Wesley preached, "He did not force you; but, being assisted by his grace, you, like Mary, chose the better part."[22] Elsewhere Wesley declared, "The grace or love of God, whence cometh our salvation, is FREE IN ALL, and FREE FOR All."[23] By this joyous conviction Wesleyans live and evangelize.

This salvation flows entirely from God's grace, not from human works or merit (Eph. 2:8-9). God offers it to all people, but not all people receive it (John 1:11-13). Some reject God's invitation to salvation (Matt. 22:1-3).[24] God wants all to be saved, Wesley preached, and while God will empower our broken human will to respond to his offer of salvation, he permits humans to resist his grace, to reject the favor of his invitation.[25] God graciously seeks the redemption of everyone, but he coerces no one.[26]

The spirit and vision of John 3:16 compel those who identify as Wesleyan: "For God so loved the *world* that he gave his one and only Son, that *whoever* believes in him shall not perish but have eternal life" (NIV, emphasis added). Our loving God, by his gracious Spirit, ever reaches out to invite *each* person into fellowship with him. As Article VII in the Articles of Faith of the Church of the Nazarene states, "We believe that the grace of God through Jesus Christ is freely bestowed upon *all* people, enabling *all who will* to turn from sin to righteousness" (emphasis added).[27]

IN CHRIST

Recent scholarship on the New Testament election passages (e.g., John 15:16; Rom. 8:28-30; Eph. 1:4-5; 1 Pet. 1:5) has refocused the discussion.[28] Instead of the words "foreknew" or "predestined" in Ephesians 1:3-10, scholars have turned their attention to "in him," "in Christ."[29] This phrase, "in Christ," provides the key that unlocks the puzzle of the seeming tension in Scripture between "universal" passages (Christ died for the salvation of all persons) and "particular" passages (God chose only some for salvation). This means that Christ, chosen "before the creation of the world" (v. 4, NIV; John 1:1), is God's "elect" One (1 Pet. 2:6; Luke 9:35). God chose, appointed, elected, Christ as the "corporate" head of all humanity, the Redeemer of the World. Christ stands as the representative head of the covenant people of Israel and of the church.[30] In Christ, Paul declares, all the promises of God were fulfilled (2 Cor. 1:20).

As the representative of all, Christ died for all. As the head of a new humanity, Christ leads the way into resurrection life. Paul tells the Roman Christians: "Consequently, just as one trespass resulted in condemnation for all people, so also one righteous act resulted in justification and life for all people. For just as through the disobedience of the one man the many were made sinners, so also through the obedience of the one man the many will be made righteous" (Rom. 5:18-19, NIV).

To participate in the Father's "elected One," to become one with him through faith (Gal. 3:26-28), one must enter into Christ (2 Cor. 5:17; Eph. 4:24) by new birth through the Holy Spirit (John 3:3-6).[31] Nazarene theologian Mildred B. Wynkoop observed, "Individual persons are not chosen to salvation, but it is Christ who has been appointed as the only Saviour [*sic*] of men. *The way of salvation is predestined.*"[32] Christ is that way. The Holy Spirit, through obedient faith, unites believers to Christ in his death and resurrection. The apostle Paul makes this clear in Galatians 3:26: "So in Christ Jesus you are all children of God through faith" (NIV).

Many scholars, therefore, now understand that "election" means corporate election,[33] not individual predestination. In other words, God elects not so much persons as *a people.* The doctrine of corporate election in Christ sums up the entire history of election in Scripture. It begins with Abraham, continues through the people of Israel, and proceeds on to Christ and the church.[34] In his incarnation, death, and resurrection, Christ fulfilled the election of God's people, Israel. Abraham was chosen and called out by God (elected) with the view that "all peoples on earth will be blessed through" him (Gen. 12:3, NIV). Christ now extends that blessing to the world.

Theologian Suzanne McDonald observes that God chose Israel to be God's image-bearing people, representing God to humanity and humanity to God.[35] Jesus Christ, the God-man, Israel's true Messiah, fulfilled Israel's vocation. As king, he represented the entire nation. Jesus represented ("imaged" Col. 1:15) God in the world as no other could. In his body, Christ bore Israel's rejection and the whole world's sin. In his death and resurrection, he triumphed over the powers of darkness that held humanity captive (Eph. 4:8; Col. 2:14-15; Rev. 20:7-10).[36] By that triumph, he released God's blessing to the nations and pioneered a new humanity (Heb. 12:2), a new people (the church) to represent God to the world.

As Christ sums up Israel's election, so Christ accomplishes the election of God's new people, the church. God chose, by his free will, to elect, to create the church, which consists of those united to Christ by faith.[37] "In Christ" is the key to and glorious meaning of election. No one is excluded from the invitation to participate in this new people of God. In Christ those who were "far away" are "brought near by the blood of Christ" (Eph. 2:13, NIV).

One of the images the New Testament employs to describe the relationship between Christ and his church is the image of marriage (5:25-27; Rev. 19:7-9). This reminds us once again of the wedding invitation, except now we need not wait for the invitation to arrive. Christ himself is the Bridegroom. All who are in Christ by faith compose Christ's bride, the church. No longer simply invited wedding guests, we join Christ as the center of the wedding party.

THE PURPOSE OF OUR ELECTION IN CHRIST

One question remains. What is the purpose of this glorious election in Christ? Why has God done all this? Yes, election includes forgiveness of sins and new life in Christ. But there is so much more. Israel's election involved salvation—seen in the Old Testament as deliverance from foreign powers and freedom in the promised land. But God's intention for Israel did not end there. In Genesis 12, after promising to bless Abraham, God promised, "All peoples on earth will be blessed through you" (v. 3, NIV). God always had the whole world in view.

Likewise, God elected the church with the whole world in view (Eph. 3:8-12). New Testament scholar N. T. Wright observes that God purposes "to rescue the whole creation, humankind of course centrally included, from sin and death."[38] Jack Cottrell adds, "The election of the church is election to service. The church is God's vehicle for the proclamation of the good news of redemption in Christ."[39] David J. Bosch noted that when the purpose of service "is withheld, election loses its meaning."[40] British missiologist Lesslie Newbigin put it this way, "To be elect in Christ Jesus, and there is no other election, means to be incorporated into his mission to the world, to be the bearer of God's saving purpose for the whole world."[41] Mission is the purpose of Christ's people, the church.

A bride, however much she is delighted to be engaged to her Beloved, need not ask, "Am I invited to the wedding?" Instead, she should ask, "Whom shall I invite?" And the Groom, whose resources are limitless, answers, "Invite them all!" Jesus told a parable about a king who prepared a wedding banquet for his son. He told his servants, "'Go to the street corners and invite to the banquet anyone you find.' So the servants went out into the streets and gathered all the people they could find, the bad as well as the good, and the wedding hall was filled with guests" (Matt. 22:9-10, NIV). The wedding banquet is ready. The king has instructed his servants to invite everyone, without discrimination.

Rather than bending us inward, the biblical doctrine of electing grace liberates us to turn outward to everyone and participate in God's mission to redeem the world. Jesus challenges us, as he did the disciples, to open our "eyes and look at the fields! They are ripe for harvest" (John 4:35, NIV). Jesus "is the atoning sacrifice for our sins, and not only for ours but *also* for the sins of the *whole world*." (1 John 2:2, NIV, emphasis added).

Broadcast the invitation (Matt. 22:1-10; 28:16-20)! Invite them all—"to the praise of [God's] glorious grace" (Eph. 1:5-6)!

Glennie was no theologian. As far as I know, she never debated questions about God's electing grace. But through the witness of the Christian community, Glennie experienced that grace. By their lives and their words Christians proclaimed to Glennie the good news of Christ's victory. They extended to Glennie Christ's invitation to peace with God. Gladly, Glennie accepted the invitation and trusted in Christ. Then, as a grateful witness to the gospel, she began to invite others to new life in Christ. God's free and sufficient grace—"FREE IN ALL, and FREE FOR ALL"—not only reached Glennie but also began to reach others through her.

It turns out that Glennie was on God's list after all. And so are all the other "Glennies" in the world.

Thanks be to God for his bountiful and free grace!

Questions for Consideration

1. When have you been surprised by the work of God's grace in your life or that of another?
2. If Christ died for all and wants everyone to be saved, why do some people remain not saved?
3. What are some of the biblical texts that cause you to believe the gospel is meant for everyone?
4. How was God's grace operative in your eventual conversion?

Additional Resources

Klein, William W. *The New Chosen People: A Corporate View of Election*. Rev. ed. Eugene, OR: Wipf and Stock, 2015.

Maddox, Randy L. *Responsible Grace: John Wesley's Practical Theology*. Nashville: Kingswood Books, 1994.

Olson, Roger E. *Arminian Theology: Myths and Realities*. Downers Grove, IL: IVP Academic, 2006.

Thornhill, A. Chadwick. *The Chosen People: Election, Paul and Second Temple Judaism*. Downers Grove, IL: InterVarsity Press, 2015.

Wesley, John. "Free Grace." Sermon 128. In *The Sermons of John Wesley*. Edited by Thomas Jackson. 1872. Wesley Center Online, 1999. http://wesley.nnu.edu/john-wesley/the-sermons-of-john-wesley-1872-edition/sermon-128-free-grace/.

Witherington, Ben. "Why I'm Not a Calvinist: Seven-Minute Seminary." Published on October 8, 2013. Seedbed video, 6:03. https://www.youtube.com/watch?v=KjUYw6Vg0bQ.

Wright, N. T. *The Day the Revolution Began: Reconsidering the Meaning of Jesus's Crucifixion*. New York: HarperOne, 2016.

5

THE GRACE THAT GOES BEFORE

PREVENIENT GRACE IN THE WESLEYAN TRADITION

David A. Busic, DMin

Christians often begin their conversion testimonies with declarative statements such as, "I came to Christ as a child at a vacation Bible school," or "I came to Christ during a youth camp when I was fourteen." These are honest attempts to locate a time when a divine encounter transformed one's life. However, as genuine as these testimonies are, they are theologically imprecise descriptions of what actually happens.

In a persuasive statement that describes how a person is transformed by God's grace, the apostle Paul writes, "As for you,[1] you were dead in your transgressions and sins, in which you used to live. . . . But because of his great love for us, God, who is rich in mercy, made us alive with Christ even when we were dead in transgressions—it is by grace you have been saved" (Eph. 2:1-2*a*, 4-5, NIV). Paul makes two definitive statements about the order of salvation. *First*, he declares every person to be dead in their transgressions and sins. Since spiritual "death" is nonresponsive prior to an encounter with Christ, every person is spiritually comatose, insensitive. *Second*, since dead people cannot respond, no spiritually dead person can "come to Christ" in his or her own strength. Help must come from outside. And so, into this desperate situation, God does something for us we cannot do for ourselves. He comes to where we are. In the power of the Holy Spirit, God moves toward us.

JOHN WESLEY AND PREVENIENT GRACE

The Wesleyan-Holiness tradition fully embraces the optimism of grace that reaches all persons. This is expressed in John Wesley's understanding of "preventing" or "prevenient" grace.[2] From birth, God's grace is active in all persons, seeking to draw them to eternal life in Jesus Christ. This is true even if they have never heard the gospel proclaimed. God's prior presence and action through the Holy Spirit is "prevenient grace," the grace that "goes before" (Lat., *prae-veniens*, "going before") hearing the good news, spiritual awakening, and conversion.[3] No person is a stranger to God's grace, and everyone is the object of the Spirit's wooing. As fallen human beings, judged by God to be "dead in [our] transgressions and sins" (Eph. 2:1, NIV), we are incapable of coming to God in our own strength. Therefore, God is always the first one on the scene of all awakening and conversion. The initial activity of the Holy Spirit is "prevenient" because it always precedes our response. One may come to faith in Jesus Christ, but no one ever comes to Christ unless God draws and enables him or her by his Spirit. Jesus told his disciples that would be the work of the Holy Spirit (John 14:16-27; 15:26; cf. 6:44).

John Wesley was adamant, if not redundant, on this point. Renowned Wesley scholar Albert Outler wryly observes, "[Wesley] insisted almost tediously, the initiative is with God, the response is with [humans]."[4] God is always the initiator in the divine-human relationship, and God's grace always precedes human response. Thus prevenient grace is God's way of preparing a person's heart and mind for saving and justifying grace. As Lovett Weems puts it, "God seeks us before we ever seek God. The initiative of salvation is with God from the very beginning. Before we ever take a step, God is there."[5] Consequently, while not irresistible, no person is left without the offer of restorative grace. For those in the Wesleyan-Holiness tradition, this means that a Christian never encounters a "morally neutral context"[6] when sharing the gospel with someone. There is no person we meet who has not been affected by prevenient grace. "Such is the seriousness of God's purpose that he will exercise every opening given him to draw people to himself."[7]

That is not to say Wesley believed in different classifications of grace, such as prevenient, justifying, sanctifying, sustaining, sufficient, and so on.[8] Grace is not to be dissected into categorical measures or types of distribution. As Jack Jackson points out, "God's grace is singular,"[9] or, from Wesley himself, God's grace is simply "the love of God."[10] Wesley focused on the experiential nature of God's grace.

> Depending on their stage of discipleship, people experience God's grace differently. Those in the state of nature experience grace preveniently; once awakened, they experience grace in a convincing and justifying manner; and then, finally, once they are justified, they experience grace working to sanctify their hearts and minds.[11]

Nazarene theologian Mildred Bangs Wynkoop became a major theological voice within the Holiness Movement. She was influential in helping the Church of the Nazarene rediscover its Wesleyan roots. One of her important contributions was to show that Wesley's theological accent upon Christian holiness had more to do with the free grace of God than with a person's free will. In her work *Foundations of Wesleyan-Arminian Theology*, Wynkoop writes, "Wesley's emphasis was not on free will, as is so often supposed. His emphasis was on free grace, or prevenient grace, granted to any and all men and accounting for all the good found in the world."[12] Wesleyans should speak of "*freed will*," the will empowered, set free, by the Holy Spirit, which makes it possible for a person actively to confess faith in Jesus Christ as Redeemer. For Wesleyans, all the way through, salvation is of God, by grace alone.[13]

Wynkoop differentiates the Wesleyan understanding of prevenient grace from the Calvinistic doctrine of common grace. God's intention has always been to lavish his creation with love and does nothing except for the flourishing of life. But while common grace is God's undeserved favor granted to all and given to benefit the whole creation, it does not lead to salvation. Grace that leads to salvation is reserved for the elect alone. But for Wesleyans the goal of prevenient grace, extended to everyone, is to awaken a person to the offer of salvation and lead him or her to repentance and to eternal life in Christ. This is a consequential distinction because it places the work of saving grace—and, later, sanctifying grace—squarely on the activity of God, rather than primarily on a person's will or personal decision. "Any good in a man is only by the free grace of God."[14] Thus, even though God chooses not to force an obedient response, the agency begins and ends with God.

Karl Barth, eminent twentieth-century Swiss Reformed theologian, taught that election means God eternally "elects" to be Father, Son, and Holy Spirit. And the Father elects the Son to be the Redeemer through the power of the Holy Spirit. The Son is God's "elect one." Election "depends wholly and utterly upon . . . the election of Jesus Christ."[15] "The Father loves the Son and the Son is obedient to the Father. In this love and obedience God gives Himself to man. He takes upon himself man's lowliness in order that man may be exalted."[16] God's offer of salvation through Jesus, by the Holy Spirit, is intended for everyone; all persons are "elect," chosen for salvation in Jesus Christ. But as the Bible makes clear, "There is no election [of man] which cannot be followed by rejection, no rejection which cannot be followed by election."[17]

John Wesley and Karl Barth are in essential agreement. God has elected or chosen for everyone to participate in the fullness of God's life. He desires that everyone be conformed to the image of God's Son. "The grace or love of God," Wesley proclaimed, "whence cometh our salvation, is FREE IN ALL, and FREE FOR ALL."[18] An essential part of this "election" is that God provides the capacity for humans to respond positively. But God's offer is not coercive. By its nature, reciprocal love requires freedom to accept or reject. Thus prevenient grace not only goes before our response to the offer of salvation but also enables a response to the Spirit's prompting and wooing.

We do not initiate redemption. But enabled by the Spirit, we can actively respond. God chooses us so that we can choose God.

The Gospel of Luke tells the story of a shepherd with one hundred sheep (Luke 15:3-7). Ninety-nine of them are safe in the pen. Rather than cut his losses, and make the prudent decision to be content with ninety-nine sheep accounted for, the shepherd leaves the ninety-nine to search for the one lost sheep. The shepherd is unsatisfied until the lost one is found and brought safely to the fold. This beautiful parable reveals the heart of God and the nature of prevenient grace. When lost sheep cannot come home, the Good Shepherd seeks them and brings them home. The Shepherd's yearning is sheer grace, motivated by his concern for the well-being of the lost one.

Jesus later provides a one-verse summary of the gospel of free grace: "For the Son of Man came to seek and to save the lost" (Luke 19:10, NIV). That is the order of redemption and the beginning of discipleship. God initiates—we respond.

WORKING *OUT* WHAT GOD IS WORKING *IN*

The entire New Testament bears witness, and the apostle Paul's writings especially emphasize, that "when a person has come to faith in Jesus as the risen Lord, that event is itself a sign of the Spirit's work through the gospel, and that, if the Spirit has begun that 'good work' of which that faith is the first fruit, you can trust that the Spirit will finish the job."[19] But this doesn't remove the importance of human participation; relationship entails cooperation.

Philippians 1:6 says, "Being confident of this, that he who began a good work in you will carry it on to completion until the day of Christ Jesus" (NIV). Moreover, believers must "continue to work out [their] salvation with fear and trembling, for it is God who works in [them] to will and to act in order to fulfill his good purpose" (2:12*b*-13, NIV). We must, by grace, work *out* in the church and the world what God is working *in* us.

Biblical examples abound. God came to Abraham in a place called Ur of the Chaldeans (now called Iran). God initiated the call:

I will make you into a great nation,
  and I will bless you;
I will make your name great,
  and you will be a blessing.
I will bless those who bless you,
  and whoever curses you I will curse;

and all peoples on earth
will be blessed through you. (Gen. 12:2-3, NIV)

Who went first? God did. Who began the good work in Abraham? God did. But Abraham had to respond in obedience to work *out* in the world what God was working *in* him.

God came to Jacob in a dream revealing a stairway to heaven (28:10-22). God came to him again and wrestled with Jacob at the Jabbok River (32:22-32). Who went first? God did. Who began the good work in Jacob? God did. But Jacob had to work *out* what God was working *in* him.

Moses was one hundred miles from nowhere. God came to him through a burning bush and called him to rescue his people from Egyptian slavery (Exod. 3:1–4:17). Who went first? God did. Who began the good work in Moses? God did. But Moses had to work *out* what God was working *in* him.

The living Christ appeared to Saul (or assaulted him) on the road to Damascus (Acts 9:1-19). Saul was not searching for God; he was on a mission to persecute Christians. Who went first? God did. Who began the good work in Saul who soon became Paul, missionary to the Gentiles? God did. But as Paul would later say in his letter to the Philippian church, he had to work *out* what God was working *in* him.

The Ethiopian eunuch on a desert road (Acts 8), Cornelius through a vision at three in the afternoon (Acts 10), Lydia by a riverside (Acts 16)—what do they share in common? These and many more stories like them show people responding in faith to God who first came to them. All of them were working *out* what God was working *in* them.

There is a consistent pattern of God acting through grace and people responding in obedient faith. British missiologist Lesslie Newbigin famously said, “Faith is the hand that grasps the finished work of Christ and makes it my own.” It does not remove the need for a response, but prevenient grace always comes first. Even Augustine, who was a steadfast proponent of predestination, affirmed, “He that made us without ourselves, will not save us without ourselves.”[20]

PROVIDENCE AND PREVENIENCE

There is a difference between providential grace and prevenient grace. Providence is how God provides for the sustenance and provision of his creation.[21] God "sees to" (Gen. 22:8, 14) what is needed to sustain the world and to provide for individual persons. How God's providence affects each person's life is profoundly mysterious. When and where and into what family one is born is a question of providence. Why one person is born into a Hindu family in India in 1765 and another person is born into a Christian family in Canada in 2015 are matters of providence. God's providence carries varying degrees of spiritual responsibility. One born into a devout Christian family will be held to more stringent account than one born into a Buddhist environment. One who is given opportunity to hear the gospel throughout life will be judged differently from someone who has never heard the name of Jesus.

Jesus's parable of the faithful and wise servant is about more than material possessions; it involves stewardship of God's grace. "From everyone who has been given much, much will be demanded; and from the one who has been entrusted with much, much more will be asked" (Luke 12:48, NIV). Not all are given equal opportunity and the same ground on which to stand. Some are given more, and some are given less. With the gift of "more" comes an increased requirement for return and response. These are matters of divine providence.

If providence is where God places us, prevenience is the multifaceted ways God meets us. Everyone receives the same grace that goes before salvation. But opportunities for response differ. Nevertheless, God extends himself to everyone, persistently and patiently. This distinguishes Christianity from other world religions that teach that if humans first move toward God, God will respond. Christianity reverses the order; God always acts first, thereby enabling response. God initiates the good work of grace and peace. Redemption and new creation always begin with God's initiative. Nothing reveals this more than the conviction that the Father sent Jesus Christ into the world. God always acts first. The Holy Spirit awakens persons to their need for salvation, convicts them of sin, and applies the atonement of Christ as they respond in faith. For John Wesley, spiritual awakening is more than mere conscience:

> There is no man, unless he has quenched the Spirit, that is wholly devoid of the grace of God. No man living is entirely destitute of what is vulgarly called *natural conscience*. . . . Every one has some measure

> of that light . . . which . . . enlightens every man that cometh into the world. And every one . . . feels more or less uneasy when he acts contrary to the light of his own conscience. So that no man sins because he has not grace, but because he does not use the grace which he hath.[22]

An uneasy conscience, an increasing awareness of right and wrong, and awakening spiritual awareness are God's gracious gifts to everyone. This confidence has important implications for evangelism in the Wesleyan spirit.

PREVENIENT GRACE AND EVANGELISM

I once met with a group of Christian pastors who live where it is very difficult to follow Christ. It is not illegal to be a Christian, but there are stringent national laws against proselytizing from one faith to another. Overt Christian evangelism is severely punished by imprisonment and even death. I asked the pastors how evangelism happens in such a hostile and dangerous environment. After a few moments of silence, a pastor answered, "Dreams." I did not understand, so I asked him to explain. "Not dozens, but hundreds of our neighbors are having dreams in the night. The risen Christ appears to them in all of his beauty and majesty. When they awake, they come asking questions. 'Tell us about this man who comes to us in the night.' When they ask, it is our obligation to answer. We are not evangelizing; we are merely bearing witness to their own experiences. Many of them are committing their lives to Christ in that way."

In places where the church is facing closed doors, the Spirit of God is going ahead of us. The prevenient grace of God knows no impenetrable boundaries or barriers. The love of God relentlessly reaches even the most difficult, resistant, and hostile persons. They may never respond in obedient faith, but they cannot escape the pervasive presence of the God who will not stop loving and drawing them.

That has been the repeated story of the *JESUS* film. The movie dramatically recounts the life of Christ. It has been an effective instrument of grace in the lives of multiplied thousands around the world. It has been shown to people in remote areas where the name of Jesus has never been spoken. Sometimes the chief of a tribe will stand in the middle of the showing and say, "Stop! We know this man. He appeared to our ancestors many years ago and revealed this story of salvation. He said one day someone would come to tell us his name. And now we know his name is Jesus." As is always the case, the Spirit of God is far ahead of the church. The Holy Spirit had been cultivating the soil of their hearts to receive the gospel. Prevenient grace had intersected with God's providential design long before the church arrived to proclaim the good news. As a result, often an entire tribe puts its faith in Christ.

Christian evangelism is neither a solo act nor a solitary moment. It happens in relational interactions prompted by the Holy Spirit, who always graciously goes before. No Christian can look in life's rearview mirror and fail to see the marvelous ways God has acted to awaken and bring him or her to repentance and faith in Christ Jesus.

My friend Stephane was an atheist, attending a university in Germany, where he was studying robotic science. His atheist uncle told him about a movie called *The Mission.* He encouraged Stephane to watch the movie because of its "impeccable acting and beautiful landscapes." The movie is set in the eighteenth century, in the northeastern Argentinian jungle. A Spanish Jesuit mission has been established to reach the Guarani indigenous tribes for Christ. Stephane rented the movie. He was especially moved by a scene where a slave trader and mercenary named Rodrigo Mendoza[23] climbs a steep mountain waterfall. Strapped to his back are the tools of his trade, his armor and his swords. He is doing penance for his many sins. As Mendoza reaches the top of the precipice, a warrior from the tribe Mendoza had kidnapped and sold into slavery jumps toward him, holding a knife as if to cut Mendoza's throat. After hesitating a moment, the tribesman cuts the rope from Mendoza's shoulders and sends the heavy pack tumbling to the bottom of the waterfall.

Mendoza is suddenly aware that something has changed this young warrior from being thirsty for vengeance to being willing to show mercy. Exhausted and covered with mud, Mendoza falls to the ground. He begins to weep tears, not of remorse, but of joy born of inner peace. He is given sanctuary in the village and welcomed into the community. Eventually Mendoza takes the vows of a Jesuit priest.

Later, Mendoza is given a book from which he reads a passage on the meaning of love. Stephane did not know the source of the words but said they were the most poetic and beautiful words he had ever heard. They so captured him that he watched the scene repeatedly and meticulously. He wrote down the words so as not to forget them. He then went to a library to research the poem's source. To his surprise, the words were from the Bible. For the first time, Stephane held a Bible. He repeatedly read 1 Corinthians 13, the "love chapter."

Not long afterward, Stephane became romantically interested in a fellow college student. One night she invited Stephane to a club. It turned out to be a Bible study. Stephane learned the Our Father prayer (the Lord's Prayer). As a scientist, he believed in experimentation to determine logical outcomes. He discovered that each time he prayed the Our Father before going to bed, he would rest peacefully. Soon he began to pray before bed each night. He was being awakened by a pursuing love and grace "going ahead."

The missionary God began to answer the prayers of a young atheist. He had discovered the splendor of God's love through a movie containing "impeccable acting and beautiful landscapes." Stephane responded to the "grace that goes before." He confessed faith in Christ and began to work *out* in the world what God was working *in* him. Stephane is now a missionary in the Church of the Nazarene. He oversees the education and preparation of pastors for an entire region. Such is the prevenient grace of God that leads to repentance and transformation.

Belief in the power of prevenient grace makes it impossible to despair of anyone who has not yet become a Christian. We must never give up hope for anyone, because God has not. The confidence of an evangelist rests neither in the evangelist nor in the ability of the one hearing the gospel. Rather, our absolute confidence is that God's love is for everyone. It is extravagant (Eph. 1:7), relentless, and unchangeable. It is sufficient to complete what God begins.

Questions for Consideration

1. What are some of the ways God's prevenient grace was operative in leading you to Christian discipleship?
2. How might Christians aid God's prevenient grace operative in the lives of persons who are not Christians?
3. How might they obstruct prevenient grace?

4. Is the Holy Spirit actually drawing all persons to faith, even when it appears that nothing of this sort is happening?

Additional Resources

Crofford, J. Gregory. *Streams of Mercy: Prevenient Grace in the Theology of John and Charles Wesley*. Asbury Theological Seminary Series: The Study of World Christian Revitalization Movements in Pietist/Wesleyan Studies 3. Lexington, KY: Emeth Press, 2010.

Klein, William W. *The New Chosen People: A Corporate View of Election*. Rev. ed. Eugene, OR: Wipf and Stock, 2015.

Payk, Christopher. *Grace First: Christian Mission and Prevenient Grace in John Wesley*. Tyndale Studies in Wesleyan History and Theology. Toronto: Clements Academic, 2015.

Shelton, W. Brian. *Prevenient Grace: God's Provision for Fallen Humanity*. Anderson, IN: Warner Press, 2014.

Wesley, John. "The Scripture Way of Salvation." Sermon 43. In *The Sermons of John Wesley*. Edited by Thomas Jackson. 1872. Wesley Center Online, 1999. http://wesley.nnu.edu/john-wesley/the-sermons-of-john-wesley-1872-edition/sermon-43-the-scripture-way-of-salvation/.

6

JUST JUSTIFICATION?

FORGIVENESS WITH A WELCOME

Timothy R. Gaines, PhD

In this chapter we turn to the doctrine of justification by grace through faith alone.[1] We will explore how a distinctly Wesleyan approach to this doctrine offers guidance for how Wesleyans should engage in evangelism. Briefly stated, the doctrine of justification speaks to God's forgiveness of humans and what God does when declaring them righteous. Justification involves what it means to be reconciled to God (2 Cor. 5:18-20; Col 1:21-23) through the victory of Jesus on the cross and his resurrection and what it means to be introduced to new life in him (2 Cor. 5:17; Gal. 3:26; Phil. 3:7-11). Because all of this is the work of God alone (Phil. 3:9), we humans engage in and appropriate it simply by trusting in what God has accomplished in Christ by the Spirit to forgive and justify us. That trust is what we often call faith, which is itself God's gift.

THE CORRECT QUESTION?

To see how a Wesleyan understanding of justification will be helpful, let's begin with a story.

"Are you saved?" An earnest volunteer knelt beside me on the field of Qualcomm Stadium in San Diego at the conclusion of a service in what would be Billy Graham's last evangelism crusade. "You should probably go forward, just to be sure," he said, motioning to the front of the platform where hundreds of people who had streamed from their seats were gathering for prayer at the aged evangelist's invitation. "Well, I'm in training to be a pastor," I gingerly attempted to explain, before he spoke again. "That doesn't matter. You should go down, just to be sure that you're saved."

For the rest of the evening and for years to come I wondered about the man's question. If I understood him correctly, he believed justification and salvation mean the same thing. For him, justification seemed to be the sum of salvation. At any rate, his question raises the question of how our understanding of justification affects our practice of evangelism. That is a question we Wesleyans must address for two reasons.

First, a Wesleyan vision of salvation makes us somewhat distinct in the Christian family. We believe that justification is a vitally important aspect of salvation but also that salvation is *more* than being justified. For Wesleyans, justification opens the door to further transformation. It is one of the more beautiful and compelling aspects of who we are; it is a message of hope worth offering to the world.

The *second* reason is to make sure our understanding of salvation affects how we practice evangelism.

First, let's discuss the meaning of justification by grace through faith. This will provide a springboard for knowing how to practice evangelism. Let's use a metaphor: justification, understood in a Wesleyan way, is like an invitation to receive hospitality. Recall a time when you received a gracious invitation that shaped you in an unmistakable way. Invitations to social gatherings might come to mind at first. But they merely point toward what I have in mind. A dinner lasts one evening, and it doesn't necessarily signal there will be an ongoing relationship between those who were invited and those who invited. What I have in mind is more like an admission letter to a university (with a full scholarship, of course!). It extends an invitation to *join a community that will forever change you.* Adoption also resembles justification as Wesleyans understand it. An invitation to become a new member of a family doesn't end with the invitation and an initial acceptance; it opens to new depths of love, commitment, community, and transformation.

The metaphor of justification as an invitation to receive God's hospitality is consistent with Jesus's teaching and the Wesleyan hope of salvation. There is more. If justification is like an invitation to hospitality, then we in the Wesleyan tradition should be well prepared for evangelism. Hospitality is characteristically important for us.[2] If justification is understood as an invitation to God's hospitality, then our congregational hospitality can help us understand justification and the larger doctrine of salvation.

JUST JUSTIFICATION?

If the metaphor of hospitality seems an odd way to describe justification, it's probably because justification is most often described in legal terms. By "legal" is meant the relationship between guilt and innocence as seen in the following illustration. Imagine you have committed a crime and are being tried in court. You know you are guilty. There are witnesses, even video evidence. You have even entered a guilty plea. By committing the crime, your relationship with the rest of society has been violated, fractured. The judge and jury hear the testimony of the witnesses. Your guilt is not in question. At the conclusion of the trial the judge says, "I know you are guilty. You have grossly violated your responsibility to me and to society. You therefore deserve to pay the penalty." But somehow in a surprise move, the judge says, "Because I am a gracious judge, I am going to render a verdict of 'not guilty.' I am going to consider you innocent."

According to the illustration, there's nothing you can do to deserve such a surprising and happy verdict. It is a sheer act of grace. Your guilt has been expunged. Your violated relationship will be set right again, but only because the judge has been gracious to you.

There is biblical warrant for describing justification in legal terms. When Paul discusses justification, especially in Romans and Galatians, the legal implications are plain. The Greek word Paul uses for justification was used to describe legal proceedings where the accused are declared innocent.

Augustine, the great fourth-century theologian, developed a doctrine of original sin that set the tone for the sixteenth-century Protestant Reformation. According to Augustine, all humans are born into a state of guilt and are therefore in need of justification, forgiveness. For him, there is nothing we can do to justify ourselves before God. Salvation is a gift of God's grace precisely because it is a gift to those who *cannot* help themselves. We are all guilty, and so for Augustine, salvation is a gift; there is nothing we can do to earn it.[3]

When a British monk named Pelagius (ca. AD 360–ca. AD 418) suggested there remains in us a spark of goodness that allows us to choose to be saved in our own strength, of our own will, Augustine spared no energy in refuting him. If there were good in us that could contribute to our salvation, Augustine argued, that would amount to our saving ourselves, or at least contributing to our salvation. Augustine insisted that *anything* that is good in us comes as a gift of grace. Faith itself is a gift from God. Salvation is entirely God's doing. Even our desire for salvation is God's gift.

As the Reformation began, the legal understanding of justification dominated. Martin Luther (1483–1546) picked up Augustine's themes. The doctrine of justification by grace through faith alone became a Reformation hallmark. The Protestant Reformers rejected the idea that salvation can be earned or purchased in any measure. We contribute nothing to our salvation; it is by grace through faith alone.

Fifteen hundred years after Paul wrote to the Romans and Galatians, Luther penned his own pastoral letter. We are justified, Luther taught, by faith in the "infinite righteousness" of Christ that "swallows up all sins in a moment."[4] The Word of God is the word of the gospel. The one "who trusts in Christ exists in Christ." And since "it is impossible that sin should exist in Christ," it is Christ's righteousness that covers up human unrighteousness.[5] For Luther, no amount of religious activity or rule keeping can make us righteous before God. As we trust that Christ's righteousness covers our unrighteousness, we are clothed in the innocence of the crucified and resurrected Jesus. "God's mercy alone," Luther correctly insisted, “works everything, and our will [contributes] nothing, but is rather the subject of Divine working, else all will not be ascribed to God.”[6]

John Calvin (1509-64), who had studied law, was fond of justification as a legal metaphor.[7] He compared God to an impartial judge who presides over the examination of one who has been charged as a criminal. A person is justified by faith, Calvin writes, when he or she “grasps the righteousness of Christ through faith, and clothed in it, appears in God’s sight not as a sinner but as a righteous man.”[8]

For the Reformers, justification means being held inside Christ’s righteousness when we have none of our own. By grace through faith, Christ’s righteousness is bestowed upon us; we contribute nothing to earn or deserve it.

John Wesley (1703-91), following Luther and Calvin, also taught that we contribute nothing to our justification before God. “I believe justification by faith alone, as much as I believe there is a God. . . . I have never varied from it, no, not a hair’s breadth from 1738 to this day.”[9] “The plain scriptural notion of justification is pardon,” Wesley instructs. He is appealing to a legal concept.[10] Against some in his day who thought we can and must live holy lives before being counted righteous by God, Wesley insisted that our justification is a sheer gift of grace. Faith—God’s gift—is the only necessary condition for being justified. We can do nothing to earn it! Our faith, Wesley insisted, must be placed in Christ, in what he accomplished on the cross. Such faith enables us to rest from our anxious labors of attempting to earn our justification. Faith, Wesley says, is the “sole condition of justification.”[11]

Wesley also agreed with Augustine that there is no goodness in us that allows us even to initiate our salvation. Even the *desire* for salvation, Wesley contended, is a gift of God’s grace that awakens in us a longing for God. Being justified by God, then, is entirely God’s doing. By faith, we trust that God has done all that is necessary for us to be justified, precisely because there is nothing we can do. Like a person who steps onto an elevated platform and, with arms crossed across the chest and eyes closed, falls backward, trusting that friends below will break his or her fall, for Wesley justification by faith is a “trust fall” into the sure merits of Christ.

But as important as justification is for Wesleyans, it is not the only aspect of salvation. That is why salvation must never be limited to legal metaphors or terms. This is also true for Augustine, Luther, and Calvin. Each of them affirmed, in their own way, that God's salvation does more than simply erase our guilt. In that respect, John Wesley joins them. But the Wesleyan tradition adds an accent to the importance of the ongoing work God accomplishes beyond justification. According to the Wesleyan view of salvation, justification opens the door to much more—to new creation, to transformation in the image of Christ. While justification certainly includes what God has done to overcome the distorted relationship between us and God caused by sin, it is an entry point into lifelong transformation.

As we've seen, the Western wing of the Christian faith (through Augustine, Luther, and Calvin) tended to emphasize legal metaphors. The Wesleyan tradition, though, doesn't flow only from the West. Being familiar with Christian thought from the Eastern (Orthodox) wing of Christianity, Wesley incorporated some of its central themes, namely healing and restoration. Both of these are prevalent in the Orthodox theologies of salvation. Wesley incorporated them into his own pastoral theology.[12] According to this understanding of salvation, God is renewing, healing, and restoring the image and likeness of God in us that has been severely distorted in the fall. God's work of redemption is a present and ongoing restoration. Think of it this way: God's grace is a healing *salve* in the work of *salv*ation.[13]

A Wesleyan theology of salvation, then, can't be reduced to justification alone, as if justification is no more than a change in one's legal status before God, a change that makes one "fit for heaven" at death. Wesley affirmed that in the moment a person is justified, that person is already a new creation. In the Wesleyan way of understanding, salvation is for *now* and for the *life to come*. It combines the Western notion of justification with the Eastern emphasis on lifelong renewal. It recognizes that Christian salvation surely offers us everlasting life but that everlasting life begins now, in Christ, as we respond to God's grace. Life in Christ *is* eternal life (John 3:36; 17:3; 1 John 5:13).

So while Wesleyans fully recognize the need for forgiveness and reconciliation with God, we don't reduce salvation to justification by faith. For Wesleyans, salvation is not only "getting saved" but also "being healed."

Let's return to the question asked of me at the conclusion of Billy Graham's sermon: "Are you saved?" I give that sincere man the benefit of the doubt. He wanted me to be clothed in the righteousness of Christ and counted righteous before God. These are good things to be sure! But encouraging me to go forward "just to be sure" suggests that for him one's justification is the most important goal of evangelism. For him, it appeared, salvation is reducible to *just* justification. For him, it seemed, salvation *is* justification. Salvation amounts to moving a person from the status of "not saved" to "saved," something like being moved from one box to another, from one category to another. Life might not look much different than it did before, except that one now has a different eternal destiny awaiting him or her. But in this life the "justified" person might remain largely in bondage to sin's power.

Wesleyans are among those who believe justification introduces Christians to the transforming power of the Holy Spirit, equipping them for increasing formation in the image of Christ. Justification is the point at which believers embrace God's gracious invitation to be transformed and then plunge into the depths of transforming grace. "You have been set free from sin and have become slaves of God," Paul reminds those under his pastoral care. "The benefit you reap leads to holiness, and the result is eternal life" (Rom. 6:22, NIV). Wesleyans embrace the fullness of salvation Paul has described. This is much more than being shifted from one "box" or "status" or "category" to another. There is a grace-enabled change from slaves to sin to servants of God; he has delivered believers "from the power of darkness and transferred [them] into the kingdom of [God's] beloved Son" (Col. 1:13, NRSV). By grace, believers are qualified "to share in the inheritance of the saints in the light" (v. 12, NRSV). The change leads into a life of Christian holiness and eternal life (Rom. 8:9-11; Col. 1:9-23).

To be clear, evangelism does involve seeking to lead people to faith in Jesus Christ, to conversion, to justification by grace through obedient faith. Receiving the good news of Jesus Christ includes justification, reconciliation with God. The joy of the gospel is that all prodigals can through Jesus Christ return to the welcoming Father. We just need to be clear that justification is the gateway to *more* of God's salvation goodness! As noted earlier, justification means accepting God's gracious invitation and stepping into unending transformation in Christ's image. "Something begins in justification," Mildred Wynkoop reminds us, "that has no ceiling."[14]

HOLY HOSPITALITY: FORGIVENESS WITH A WELCOME

This is why hospitality is such an appropriate metaphor for justification and for the practice of evangelism. The parables of Jesus often use themes of hospitality. While celebrating a meal with some Pharisees, Jesus taught them to "invite the poor, the crippled, the lame, the blind, and you will be blessed" (Luke 14:13-14, NIV). He told of a king who invited guests to a banquet. When they declined the invitation, the king invited those Jesus had instructed the Pharisees to include. "Go out to the roads and country lanes and compel them to come in, so that my house will be full" (v. 23, NIV). Entering the kingdom Jesus proclaimed comes by way of accepting a wide and lavish invitation. The banquet hall is full because the invitation is offered indiscriminately.

Jesus didn't often use the term "justification" to describe reconciliation with God. But he used it once to speak of a penitent tax collector—supposedly not welcomed by God because of his occupation—being freely welcomed (justified) in the temple by God (18:14).

Perhaps the most vivid account of "justification" in Jesus's parables is the story of the lost son in Luke 15. Here we see a striking vision of a forgiving father embracing a wayward but returning son and extending to him a lavish welcome. The son's confession is strikingly similar to the prayers of all who seek God's forgiveness and reconciliation (justification): "Father, I have sinned against heaven and against you" (v. 21, NIV). The father's response is to clothe his son in a robe and welcome him in celebration. Being clothed or robed in Christ's righteousness is a common metaphor for justification. But in the parable of the prodigal son, the robe is associated with being welcomed to festal celebration. The father's welcome drew the son into the father's household, where, the parable indicates, the forgiven son continued to live in reconciliation with his father. Notice that the father did not simply "consider" his son righteous; he extended a welcome to life in the father's house. Indeed, the son was not only forgiven but also welcomed and transformed.

Although the welcome might not be as obvious as in the parable of the prodigal son, another biblical account displays God's gracious invitation, his hospitality. It also shows how God welcomes us into his own life of love! John tells of Jesus appearing to the disciples in his resurrected body. He speaks to the apostle Thomas. "Reach out your hand and put it into my side" (John 20:27, NIV). That Jesus would invite Thomas to *reach into his own body* is a powerful sign of welcome. He is making room in his own body for Thomas the doubter.

Perhaps stories such as these help explain why Wesleyans are so fond of talking about *participating* in God. The apostle Peter speaks beautifully of God's invitation to participate in his life. "[God's] divine power has given us everything we need for a godly life through our knowledge of him who called us by his own glory and goodness. Through these he has given us his very great and precious promises, so that through them you may participate in the divine nature, having escaped the corruption in the world caused by evil desires" (2 Pet. 1:3-4, NIV).

Justification is the invitation *into God's own life*. He is not a closed, distant deity. Rather, God opens himself to us and invites us into his divine life of love. Begun in justification, salvation is that participation, that healing.

How might God's grand invitation shape and inform evangelism?

THE EVANGELISTIC PRACTICE OF "SOMETHING MORE"

A Wesleyan practice of evangelism proclaims that salvation joyously includes justification but is more. Beginning with the good news, justification by grace through faith alone, we invite people into God's redemptive and transforming love. John Wesley was fond of describing justification as the "door" into the house that is sanctification—a life of love.[15] Perhaps this is why John Wesley's practices of evangelism were so *hospitable*. Let's look at a few examples.

First, Wesley's practice of "field preaching" took the gospel message to people where they lived and worked, outside the walls of traditional church buildings. Field preaching was meant to "awaken" those who hear the gospel for the sake of moving them toward Christian discipleship. For Wesley, "each sermon was supposed to invite people to the next stage of

Christian discipleship."[16] He knew salvation can't be reduced to justification. A person may be awakened and justified in a moment, but God's work was only beginning. "With God's grace at work in every stage, people begin discipleship by awakening from the state of nature, experiencing initial repentance and faith in Christ that leads to justification, and *then to ongoing faith and repentance that results in holiness*."[17]

Second, Wesley organized societies, classes, and bands, groups of various sizes meant to be communities of hospitality. Persons of "every sort" who wished to grow in grace were welcome.

Third, Wesley understood the Lord's Supper, the Eucharist, in terms of Christian hospitality. Seen as a "converting ordinance," the Lord's Supper offered a point of entry into Christian discipleship and continued growth in grace. "We come to communion in our need, seeking further grace," Wesleyan theologian Randy Maddox has observed of Wesley, "not in our fitness, seeking certification."[18] Justification as having nothing of our own to offer is present in the Lord's Supper. So, too, is Communion as a means of grace. It continues to offer new horizons of growth and Christian holiness.

CONCLUSION

A Wesleyan understanding of justification as an invitation to an ongoing feast can open our imagination to practices of hospitable evangelism. Let evangelism be a matter of inviting others to a feast of grace and redemption (Matt. 22:9-10; 14:13-21). The illustrations from Wesley's ministry can be suggestive. But in each congregational context, we must find creative ways to proclaim the gospel as an invitation into God's hospitality, a hospitality that will continue to transform believers forever.

Questions for Consideration

1. What does it mean to say that we are justified by grace through faith alone?
2. Why is it important to guard against permitting "works" of any kind, including our own initiative, to be associated with justification?

3. According to a Wesleyan understanding of salvation, why is "just justification" incomplete?
4. Discuss the "First Fruits of the Spirit" in I.1-6 of John Wesley's sermon "The First Fruits of the Spirit," Sermon 8, in *The Sermons of John Wesley* (see below).

Additional Resources

Collins, Kenneth J. *The Theology of John Wesley: Holy Love and the Shape of Grace*. Nashville: Abingdon Press, 2007.

Luther, Martin. *Concerning Christian Liberty* [*On the Freedom of a Christian*]. 1520. Project Gutenberg, 2006. https://www.gutenberg.org/files/1911/1911-h/1911-h.htm.

Wesley, John. "The First Fruits of the Spirit." Sermon 8. In *The Sermons of John Wesley*. Edited by Thomas Jackson. 1872. Wesley Center Online, 1999. http://wesley.nnu.edu/john-wesley/the-sermons-of-john-wesley-1872-edition/sermon-8-the-first-fruits-of-the-spirit/.

———. "Free Grace." Sermon 128. In *The Sermons of John Wesley*. Edited by Thomas Jackson. 1872. Wesley Center Online, 1999. http://wesley.nnu.edu/john-wesley/the-sermons-of-john-wesley-1872-edition/sermon-128-free-grace/.

7

RESPECT FOR THE DIGNITY AND CONTEXTS OF ALL PERSONS

Tina Pitamber, DMin

PRESENTING THE GOSPEL WITH INTEGRITY

As believers in Jesus Christ, we have a responsibility to present the gospel with integrity. This means not adding or taking away anything from the good news, but rather recognizing that the gospel is true and has the power to transform all who repent of their sins. By presenting the gospel with integrity, we respect not only the gospel but also all persons. This includes being sensitive to another person's context.

Although the apostle Paul was a fervent evangelist, he refused to impose the gospel on others. He rejected all forms of manipulation. He insisted that the gospel be presented in a manner faithful to itself and the God of the gospel.

> Therefore, since through God's mercy we have this ministry, we do not lose heart. Rather, we have renounced secret and shameful ways; we do not use deception, nor do we distort the word of God. On the contrary, by setting forth the truth plainly we commend ourselves to everyone's conscience in the sight of God. (2 Cor. 4:1-2, NIV)

There should be no deception of any kind, no distortion of God's Word. The gospel must be presented in a manner faithful to God's character and with respect for the conscience of the hearer. Paul reminded the Thessalonian Christians, "You know what kind of men we proved to be among you for your sake. And you became imitators of us and of the Lord, for you received the word in much affliction, with joy inspired by the Holy Spirit" (1 Thess. 1:5-6, RSV).

Consistently in his Epistles, Paul was considerate of those to whom he preached. He reminded the Corinthians, "I did not come proclaiming to you the testimony of God in lofty words or wisdom" (1 Cor. 2:1, RSV). He could have but instead trusted the Holy Spirit and the power of the gospel (v. 4). He used no verbal trickery, no "brainwashing," and no dictation or manipulation that overrode a hearer's integrity. Never did Paul attempt to win persons to Jesus by intimidation or manipulative fear. He always let the beauty and power of the gospel speak for itself. By the same token, never did Paul preach as an entrepreneur anxious to accumulate customers at any price. He used no glaring lights, no "prosperity gospel," and no appeal to "the flesh." Paul respected the truth of the gospel, the character of God, and the integrity of his listeners.

Paul understood, and so should we, that it is not our job to convince others that Jesus is the Christ (1 Cor. 12:3). As Jesus had taught (John 16:7-8), he knew that to be exclusively the role of the Holy Spirit. Rather, Paul was a faithful witness, God's agent for announcing the gospel. He told the Thessalonians, "Our gospel came to you not only in word, but also in power and in the Holy Spirit and with full conviction" (1 Thess. 1:5, RSV). His presentation of Christ to them was completely free of "impure motives" and trickery; he spoke as one "approved by God" (2:3-4, NIV). Consequently, he could tell the Philippians, "What you have learned and received and heard and seen in me, do; and the God of peace will be with you" (Phil. 4:9, RSV). As witnesses today, we must follow Paul's example—respecting the dignity of all listeners, respecting contexts, and trusting the Holy Spirit.

Presenting the gospel with integrity also safeguards those who bear witness. By renouncing "disgraceful, underhanded ways" (2 Cor. 4:2, RSV), we protect our own integrity as well. We also safeguard how we are perceived by others. In his defense before Felix the Roman governor, Paul said, "I always take pains to have a clear conscience toward God and toward men" (Acts 24:16, RSV). Clearly, Paul understood that the "good news" can become "bad news" if the messenger is dishonest.

God's character is pure and true. He does not force himself upon us. He desires eternal life for us and fellowship with him, but never at the expense of our conscience. "Behold, I stand at the door and knock; if any one hears my voice and opens the door, I will come in to him and eat with him, and he with me" (Rev. 3:20, RSV). "God is love" (1 John 4:8, RSV). Love invites, woos, and sacrifices, but it does not manipulate and coerce. This is why we must present the gospel with integrity; the character of God must correctly be represented. God's love must be heard, experienced, and spoken of.

Therefore, let us be morally responsible in how we proclaim the message of Jesus Christ. This entails integrity and respect for the dignity of all persons and for their contexts.

Do diverse contexts present a hindrance to evangelism for God? Absolutely not, nor should they be for us. Diverse contexts are but opportunities for creatively presenting the gospel. Then we will be near to the heart of God.

GOD CALLS US TO EVANGELIZE ALL PEOPLE

Part of what makes the good news of Jesus Christ so exciting is that it is meant for everyone. Jesus commissioned his disciples by saying, "Therefore go and make disciples of all nations, baptizing them in the name of the Father and of the Son and of the Holy Spirit" (Matt. 28:19, NIV). That is not only an instruction but also an action statement. Jesus is instructing his disciples to invite all people to hear and obey the Word of God (v. 20).

Jesus's instructions offer hope for everyone; our God is not an exclusive or parochial God. Jesus tells us plainly, "For God so loved the world that he gave his one and only Son, that whoever believes in him shall not perish but have eternal life" (John 3:16, NIV; Rom. 10:12). Clearly, God loves all people everywhere and seeks their redemption. If that is what God intends, then as God's missionary people (the church) we must mobilize God's intentions—no exceptions.

Proclaiming the gospel to everyone is not new for Christians in the Wesleyan tradition. Because of John Wesley's conviction that the gospel is meant for all people, he looked forward to a time when God will have "put a period to sin, and misery, and infirmity, and death; and re-established universal holiness and happiness, and caused all the inhabitants of the earth to sing together, 'Hallelujah, the Lord God omnipotent reigneth!' 'Blessing, and glory, and wisdom, and honor, and power, and might, be unto our God for ever and ever!' (Rev. 7:12)."[1]

Wesley preached a sermon titled "Free Grace." His text was Romans 8:32: "He that spared not his own Son, but delivered him up for us all, how shall he not with him also freely give us all things?" (KJV). On that basis, Wesley declared, "The grace or love of God, whence cometh our salvation, is FREE IN ALL, and FREE FOR ALL."[2] He practiced what he preached by proclaiming the good news to all people, especially those excluded by the dominant culture. He sought to follow Jesus's instructions by building relationships with all people, seeking to lead them into God's kingdom of grace.

Just as John Wesley did, the church today is called to share the gospel with all people. As Christians, we must reach out to those who are different from us, the other, the unfamiliar, and the stranger.

RESPECTING CONTEXTS

This immediately raises the question, How can the church evangelize those who might be different from us? A large part of the answer lies in simply being sensitive to the Holy Spirit, who will guide us in how to reach others. We do not first need methods and strategies, as important as they may be. Rather, first we need to listen to the Holy Spirit, who will guide us.

Respecting contexts certainly includes recognizing differences. But differences must never be permitted to become obstacles to the gospel. Different contexts can include social, religious, psychological, and ethnic distinctions.

The Gospels contain examples that show Jesus's sensitivity to contexts. But not once did a different context keep him from inviting others into God's kingdom. Jesus connected with those who did not look, behave, think, or necessarily even believe as he did. Following him requires the same disposition. Remove obstructive and divisive labels; share the gospel message so that all persons can receive Jesus's gift of salvation.

Let's examine and learn from stories in the Bible that show how God extends his love and grace to people in various contexts.

Gender

In John 4:3-42 Jesus converses with a Samaritan woman. New Testament scholar Jerome H. Neyrey says we miss how unusual Jesus's conversation with her was unless we appreciate the sharp cultural stereotypes of males and females in the ancient world. In Jesus's day, the world was gender divided: males in "public" space (marketplaces, public squares, council halls, and open fields) and females in "private" space (houses, wells, and tending ovens). Jesus overcame this "space" and spoke with a "foreign" female—a Samaritan. He spoke with her at the "sixth hour." Normally women came to the well early in the morning. The "sixth hour" suggests the woman was socially ostracized by her female peers. So, in this story a female is conversing with an unrelated male, in a public place, at an unusual hour, and with someone whose fellow citizens normally scorned Samaritans.[3]

This story contains gender and religious differences. But Jesus did not let any of these keep him from bringing good news to the woman. Speaking to her, Jesus first asks for a drink. She responds, "You are a Jew and I am a Samaritan woman" (v. 9, NIV). She says this because Jews and Samaritans did not associate with each other. Jesus responds that he can give her living water. She then asks for this water (vv. 10, 15).

Jesus tells the Samaritan woman to call her husband for conversation. She responds that she doesn't have a husband (vv. 16-17). Then Jesus reveals the truth about her situation. "You are right when you say you have no husband. The fact is, you have had five husbands, and the man you now have is not your husband. What you have just said is quite true" (vv. 17-18, NIV).

Now Jesus has her attention. She recognizes that he is a prophet. Otherwise, how could he know so many details about her life? She explains that Samaritans worship in a place different from that of the Jews (v. 19). But Jesus doesn't focus on their differences. If "differences" had been the most important thing, Jesus would have walked away. Instead, he presses forward. He tells the woman what it truly means to worship God. At the same time, he criticizes the negative attitude Jews show toward Samaritans and Samaritans toward Jews.[4]

This story shows how the Holy Spirit, who attended Jesus's ministry (Luke 3:21-22; 4:1-2, 14-15), guided him in how to speak with the Samaritan woman. The Holy Spirit created the opportunity for the Samaritan woman to hear the gospel. When Jesus said she had no husband, she understood Jesus had insight from God. This caused her to listen to him. But we also learn that Jesus did not let her lifestyle, race, religion, or gender keep him from sharing God's truth with her.

Today, many women are stigmatized as socially inferior, just as was the Samaritan woman. Depending upon the cultural setting, women might be thought of as little more than sex objects, even sex slaves. They might not receive equal pay for equal work or might not be permitted to learn to read or write or even drive a car. A woman might be perceived more as an object than a person. In many ways, dignity and personhood can be denied just because someone is a woman.

The beautiful story of the Samaritan woman shows that Jesus does not offer hope and himself as Redeemer based upon gender. Everything he says to her shows respect. He offers hope and transcends the restrictive limitations of her context. In fact, because of how Jesus treats the Samaritan woman, she becomes an evangelist. She tells her village neighbors about Jesus.

Christ calls his church to reach others just as he did—to respect the person who is before us and move past arbitrary obstacles. We are to see in our presence a person, created in God's image—a candidate for God's love and redemption.

What about Those "Objectionable Sinners"?

In Luke 7:36 Jesus is invited to eat in the home of Simon, a Pharisee. While there, a disreputable woman from town learns of Jesus's presence.

Uninvited, she brings her alabaster jar of perfume into Simon's house (v. 37). Upon entering, the woman approaches Jesus and begins to wet his feet with her tears. Then she wipes them with her hair. She kisses Jesus's feet and pours perfume on them (vv. 37-38). The Pharisees respond, "If this man were a prophet, he would know who is touching him and what kind of woman she is—that she is a sinner" (v. 39). The woman's name was not on guest the list; she was a party crasher.[5] In fact, her presence was a major embarrassment for Simon.[6]

At the moment of crisis, Jesus tells a story about a moneylender and two debtors. One owed five hundred denarii (the ordinary wage of a day laborer); the other owed fifty denarii. The moneylender then forgave what they owed. Jesus asks Simon, "Which of the two will be most grateful to the moneylender?" Simon responds, "The person with the greater debt will be more grateful."

Then Jesus drives home his point. When he came into Simon's house, Simon provided no water for his feet (a sign of disrespect). By contrast, the sinful woman washed Jesus's feet with her tears. Simon did not kiss Jesus, but the sinful woman kissed Jesus's feet. Simon did not anoint Jesus's head with oil, but the sinful woman anointed Jesus's feet.[7] The sinful woman responded this way because she loved Jesus and had received his forgiveness.

If we are serious about reaching the lost, we must be like Christ. As Jesus extended himself to this woman despite her sin, we must extend ourselves to those who live differently from us, present the gospel plainly and humbly, and respect the person to whom we are speaking, including a person just like that uninvited "intruder."

Our church conducts community dinners in our city. We approach a housing complex and ask the manager if we can provide a full meal for the residents. Once we have permission, our church members volunteer time to set up, serve, and interact with the residents. Then we clean up afterward.

This is a wonderful opportunity to meet people from backgrounds different from ours. Because of what our guests tell us, we know that for many of them, life is very difficult. But that doesn't keep us from loving them. Many times they have asked, "Why are you doing this?" We respond, "We want you to know we love you and so does God."

The community dinner provides a safe place where people from different cultures, races, lifestyles, beliefs, genders, and social classes can interact without being discriminated against. Our church extends hospitality, and in return we have an opportunity to bear witness to God's love.

Religion

In the Old Testament we hear about a loving God who calls Jonah to preach repentance to a city whose religion was very different from Judaism. God instructed Jonah to go to Nineveh, the capital of Assyria. The Ninevites were bitter enemies.

The Jews worshipped one God, Yahweh; the Assyrians worshipped many gods, the chief one being Ashur. God instructed Jonah to go to Nineveh because God's care for others is universal. He wanted the people of Nineveh to repent and be forgiven.

Instead of going east to Nineveh, Jonah fled west toward Tarshish (Jon. 1:3). To get Jonah's attention, God sent a storm. After an unwanted three-day stay in the belly of a great fish, Jonah headed for Nineveh.

Jonah bitterly resented the thought of God showing mercy to the Ninevites. He was quite content for God to love the Jews, but not the evil Assyrians. As Jonah had feared, the Ninevites accepted the message of God's judgment upon their city and their sins. In fasting and sackcloth, the entire city, beginning with the king, repented. "When God saw what they did, how they turned from their evil way, God repented of the evil which he had said he would do to them; and he did not do it" (3:10, RSV).

Jonah was exceedingly angry with God (4:1). God told Jonah, "And should I not have concern for the great city of Nineveh, in which there are more than a hundred and twenty thousand people who cannot tell their right hand from their left—and also many animals?" (v. 11, NIV).

Jonah is the story of a great God of forgiveness and reconciliation, not of a great fish. Jonah was willing to preach God's judgment; he just didn't approve of God's forgiveness. He much preferred a parochial God who doesn't love universally, one who steers clear of different religious contexts. But God loves and reaches across religious barriers. Unlike Jonah, God "wants all people to be saved and to come to a knowledge of the truth" (1 Tim. 2:4, NIV). Jonah had forgotten that Israel was supposed to be "a light for the Gentiles" and was supposed to bring God's salvation "to the ends of the earth" (Isa. 49:6, NIV).

The book of Jonah confronts each of us with the question, How broad is the gospel of Jesus Christ? Does it reach across religious barriers? Are members of other religions to be loved by us? Or do we shun them?

Nabeel Qureshi was a devout Muslim.[8] Nabeel became a born-again Christian through several interactions and experiences. There were the conversations he had with his college friend David, his research of the Bible and Jesus Christ, the Christians who patiently answered his questions, and the dream given him by the Holy Spirit.

David played a crucial role in Nabeel's conversion. He patiently answered Nabeel's probing questions and debated with him over topics pertaining to the Bible, Jesus Christ, and the Qur'an. Like the apostle Paul, David did not present the gospel deceptively or coercively, but always with sensitivity to Nabeel's conscience and honest questions. David knew Nabeel was raised to believe Islam. But he did not let that become a barrier between Nabeel and himself. Instead, he respected Nabeel's dignity and context. In time, through the Holy Spirit's leading, Nabeel encountered Jesus Christ as Lord and Redeemer.

What we are learning is that through the Holy Spirit, the gospel must be presented in purity to others—respect for the gospel, the person with whom we are speaking, and the human witness.

Race

Acts 8:26-38 tells of a meeting between the apostle Philip and an Ethiopian eunuch.[9] The angel of God told Philip, "Go south to the road—the desert road—that goes down from Jerusalem to Gaza" (v. 26, NIV). On his way he met an Ethiopian man who was a minister of the Candace, queen of the Ethiopians. He had been to Jerusalem to worship and was returning home. Seated in his chariot, he was reading aloud to himself from the book of Isaiah (53:7-8). The Holy Spirit told Philip to walk beside the chariot. Upon hearing the Ethiopian, Philip asked if he understood what he was reading. "How can I," the Ethiopian replied, "unless someone explains it to me?" (Acts 8:31, NIV). Philip then explained that the text referred to Jesus, who fulfilled Isaiah's prophecy. Philip told the Ethiopian "the good news about Jesus" (v. 35, NIV). As they were traveling and conversing, the Ethiopian saw some water and asked what was to prevent him from being baptized. They "went down into the water and Philip baptized him" (vv. 34-39, NIV).

The Holy Spirit guided Philip to this Ethiopian despite their racial differences. Philip was obedient and guided the Ethiopian to conversion and Christian baptism.

As the story illustrates, ethnicity or race should never be permitted to become an obstacle to the gospel and Christian fellowship. In a world so easily polarized by racial conflict, Christians must never permit such arbitrary differences to impede or obstruct their witness to Jesus Christ and his power to redeem. It is marvelous to watch God overcoming ethnic and racial differences when Christians obey the Spirit's leading. Paul told the Galatians, "For as many of you as were baptized into Christ have put on Christ. There is neither Jew nor Greek, there is neither slave nor free, there is neither male nor female; for you are all one in Christ Jesus" (Gal. 3:28, RSV).

As we are open to the Spirit's leading, people can receive Christ, be forgiven, and become citizens of God's kingdom! The Holy Spirit did not permit ethnicity and race to become a barrier to his plans for Philip's ministry. In the same way, the Holy Spirit also wants the church to minister to persons of all racial and ethnic identities.

Toronto, Canada, where I minister, is the most racially diverse city in the world—a racial mosaic. People of numerous races live on the same street or in the same neighborhood. They work and worship together. Torontonians have learned to be sensitive to all persons in spite of their gender, religious, or racial differences.

The same must be true in the church; we must minister to and respect the dignity of all people, without any racial and ethnic bias. We are one in Christ.

Each year, statistics of the Church of the Nazarene show a growing number of multicultural churches reporting. No cultural group constitutes more than 80 percent of a worship service. This requires that we learn love and respect for diverse cultural, ethnic, and racial contexts.

Our church is located in a community where most of the people are affluent. But there is a pocket of people who live below the poverty level. To reach them, our church decided to visit the local food bank and invite its visitors to a community dinner. During our second community meal, we interacted with a person named Larry (whose racial identity differs from mine). After dinner we invited Larry to our church. He began to attend. We learned that he was going through a divorce, had lost his job, and was trying to maintain contact with his children.

Larry had little knowledge of God. But the dinner provided a setting for him to begin to learn about God. He began to read the Bible and began to realize its truth was meant for him. He confessed his sins and received Jesus Christ into his life. Today Larry is stable, has connected with his children, has remarried, and is growing in the image of Jesus Christ.

Culture and Language

The Bible shows that the good news of Jesus Christ is no respecter of cultures and languages. Genesis 11:1-9 describes people wanting to build a city and a tower that would reach to the heavens. By so doing they would "make a name for [themselves]" (v. 4, RSV). The city and tower would keep them unified and avoid their being "scattered abroad upon the face of the whole earth" (v. 4, RSV). However, God rebuked their arrogance by "[confusing] their language" and scattering them in confusion over the "all the earth" (vv. 6-8, RSV). The tower became known as Babel (confusion). By confusing the peoples' language, God rebuked their pride.

However, in Acts 2 the reverse happens.[10] On the day of Pentecost, the Holy Spirit gave the disciples the ability to proclaim the gospel in the languages of "every nation under heaven" (v. 5, RSV). Bewildered, devout men from every nation had come together after hearing the "rush of a mighty wind" signaling the outpouring of the Holy Spirit (vv. 2, 5-6). Then Peter preached his great Pentecost sermon (vv. 14-36). Those who heard Peter's proclamation of Jesus the Messiah in their own language were "cut to the heart" and asked what they should do (v. 37, RSV). "Repent, and be baptized every one of you in the name of Jesus Christ" (v. 38, RSV). Then, "those who accepted his message were baptized, and about three thousand were added to their number that day" (v. 41, NIV).

At Pentecost, God reversed the curse of Babel. The coming of the Holy Spirit made possible the gospel's proclamation in the languages and cultures of all people. Jesus can be the "light of the world" (John 8:12, NIV) because he is the "good news" for all people without regard for language or culture.

Today, for many reasons, including violence, famine, and persecution, millions of people are migrating to other parts of the world. The church must be ready to "show hospitality to strangers" (Heb. 13:1-2, NIV). Jesus said, "Then the King will say to those on his right, 'Come, you who are blessed by my Father; take your inheritance, the kingdom prepared for you. . . . I was a stranger and you invited me in'" (Matt. 25:34-35, NIV). The book of Exodus instructs, "You shall not oppress a sojourner. You know the heart of a stranger, for you were strangers in the land of Egypt" (Exod. 23:9, RSV).

During September 2017, a family from South America attended our church in Canada. A year before that, the mother of the family sent an email to me, telling me of their plan to transition to Toronto. She said they wanted to visit our church. Upon arrival, the family began to attend. They were in the process of learning a new culture, lifestyle, and language.

Our church accepted the new family wholeheartedly. We prayed for them and provided for their needs. We received them joyfully and knew it was our Christian responsibility to assist them. Although their use of English was fair, at times it was difficult for them to express themselves. Their language, culture, and lifestyle were very different from what they were experiencing in Canada. Nevertheless, our church family continued to be sensitive to their needs. Culture and language were not permitted to obstruct our ministry to them.

Jesus showed his disciples how to treat the Samaritan woman. He educated Simon the Pharisee and others about the woman who anointed Jesus's feet. God instructed reluctant Jonah to preach the word of forgiveness to foreigners. The Holy Spirit led Philip to the Ethiopian and on the day of Pentecost helped people of many cultures hear the gospel in their own languages.

If the Holy Spirit had the ability to transcend gender, sin, religion, race, and language in the past, surely he can do the same today. If we present the gospel with integrity, respect the dignity of each person and his or her context, and listen to the Holy Spirit, then there is no barrier—social class, physical ability, gender, or caste—God cannot overcome. Jesus overcomes demonic powers, sickness, and political differences. Labels don't matter to him. If we are willing to be Christ's agents, he can reach people at home and around the world.

GUIDING PRINCIPLES

This leads to an important question: How may we become sensitive to others, despite differences? There are three guiding principles that can help us be sensitive to diverse contexts.

First, See People as God Sees Them

Our dignity comes from God, not from arbitrary standards such as gender, race, and nationality. Everyone matters to God because they are made in his image (Gen. 1:26). They also matter because he loves them and gave his only Son for their salvation (John 3:16). If all people matter that much to God, then as his agents of reconciliation we must display the same. Sin alienates people from God and causes spiritual death. But the death and resurrection of Jesus Christ restores us to intimate fellowship with God.

Look at the variety of people in the Bible whom God loved: Adam and Eve, Cain the murderer, Noah the drunken man, Abraham the liar, and Jacob the deceiver. Add Rebekah the deceiver, Moses the ill-tempered, Aaron the golden-calf maker, and Rahab the prostitute. And don't forget David the adulterer, Solomon the polygynist, Peter the denier of Jesus, Paul the persecutor of Christians, and Onesimus the runaway slave. God used all of them to achieve his purposes. If we want to succeed in reaching others for Jesus Christ, we must see God's potential for all people.

So, how do we view others? By their racial identity? Their gender? Rich or poor? Educated or not? What do we see? The good news is that God doesn't look at people as some of us might. God told Samuel, "People look at the outward appearance, but the Lord looks at the heart" (1 Sam.

16:7, NIV). Samuel had made the error many of us make: he judged by appearance. Even after Pentecost, the apostle Peter had not completely learned the lesson. The apostle Paul rebuked him for failing to be faithful to the gospel (Gal. 2:11-21). Paul said that Peter had judged people by ethnic differences and had thereby nullified "the grace of God" (v. 21, RSV). Judging people by artificial distinctions is, Paul says, a form of living according to the flesh and a way of becoming agents of sin (v. 17). He warns against reconstructing walls Christ "tore down" (v. 18, RSV). To be a disciple of Christ, Paul says, requires that we die to the old sinful order of assessing and dividing people according to arbitrary barriers. The gospel of Christ and divisive walls are mutually exclusive.

Looking at people as God sees them affects how we approach evangelism. Instead of thinking we can't speak, reach out to, or love others because they are different, we should first say, "This is someone whom God loves, and we must do the same." All persons are candidates for transformation by God's grace. We must not "build up again those things which [Christ] tore down" (v. 18, RSV).

Second, God's Grace Is for All People

Once we move beyond how people look, dress, speak, eat, think, or behave, we can concentrate on what is true for all people: without Christ, everyone is spiritually dead. There is no distinction, "since all have sinned and fall short of the glory of God" (Rom. 3:23, RSV). As the Bible and human history testify, through the fall of Adam, sin has spread to all humans (5:17; Ps. 51:5). But because of Jesus Christ, sin doesn't have the final word. "If the many died by the trespass of the one man, how much more did God's grace and the gift that came by the grace of the one man, Jesus Christ, overflow to the many" (Rom. 5:15, NIV). Just as sin is common to all, the gospel of Jesus Christ is offered to all. The New Testament tells us that God is "not willing that any should perish, but that all should come to repentance" (2 Pet. 3:9, KJV). Jesus himself makes this crystal clear: "For God so loved the world that he gave his one and only Son, that whoever believes in him shall not perish but have eternal life" (John 3:16, NIV).

Third, Listen to and Obey the Holy Spirit

We must develop the habit of listening to the Holy Spirit, obeying him, and doing what he directs us to do. The Bible says the Holy Spirit knows the thoughts of the Father (1 Cor. 2:11). He also searches human hearts (Rom. 8:27) and through prevenient grace works to draw all persons to Christ (John 1:16-17; Rom. 5:20). By carefully listening to the Spirit, we will be instructed in how best to share the gospel with others. Methods for evangelism are vital. But even more important is the need to discern the Holy Spirit and be obedient to him.

The apostle Paul and others were traveling through Phrygia and Galatia (Acts 16:6-8). Their intention was to preach the gospel in Asia. But through a vision, the Holy Spirit changed their plans and sent them to the Roman province of Macedonia in Europe (vv. 9-12). Through their ministry, the church was subsequently founded in Europe. This story teaches us that the Holy Spirit can tell us what to do and what not to do. Paul and his companions were sensitive to the Holy Spirit.

Our temptation is to act first instead of first discerning God's will through prayer, searching the Scriptures, and community reflection. We will hear from God if we spend time with him. We use the principle of listening for understanding our spouse, our children, and our friends. We discern. We "hang out" with them and build a relationship. Similarly, we must "hang out" with Jesus through the Holy Spirit in prayer, services of worship, studying God's word, fasting, giving to others, and using our gifts for God. The more we hang out with Jesus, the easier it becomes to hear from him. We learn to distinguish between God's voice and other voices.

Trinity Church of the Nazarene in San Gabriel Valley, California, listened to the Spirit and began to offer free motor oil changes for single mothers in their neighborhood on Saturday mornings. Some members of the congregation were taught to change motor oil. Others ministered to single mothers while their vehicle oil was being changed. The congregation provided breakfast and lunch. Tables were provided for children to make crafts. If mothers wanted to pray, church members were prepared.

The Leonardtown, Maryland, Church of the Nazarene prayed to know how best to minister to their community. They began by building relationships with businesses and schools. They provided food for needy children. During the Christmas season the congregation placed a nativity scene on the church's lawn and then provided hot chocolate and popcorn for visitors. This congregation discerned God's will and obeyed.

Listening and obeying requires bold courage. Abraham heard God and took his family to new country. He became the father of many nations. Noah obeyed God, built an ark when there was no rain, and was saved from the flood. Moses led the Israelites out of Egypt. In the face of strong opposition, Elijah proved to the Israelites that Yahweh, not Baal, is the true God. "In the name of the Lord of Hosts" (1 Sam. 17:45, KJV), David faced and defeated Goliath and the Philistines. Esther risked her life for her people. Daniel prayed despite the law against the Jews and was spared in the company of lions. Paul and Silas were in jail, serving the gospel and singing hymns. The ground shook, and they were set free. Peter was rescued from prison by an angel. This "cloud of witnesses" (Heb. 12:1, NIV) should inspire us to listen as congregations to the Holy Spirit and then obey.

CONCLUSION

I will close with a personal story about being sensitive to the Holy Spirit. One day as I was driving home from shopping, God flashed before me the face of my sister's friend. When I arrived home, I knew I should sit and listen to God. After some time, I began to type a text message on my cell phone; it was what I thought to be a word from God. I finished typing the word "knowledge" on my phone and then asked the Lord, "Do you really want me to send this message? What if the person thinks I am crazy? What if she never speaks to my sister again?"

So I did nothing for another five minutes, debating what to do. Finally, I chose to obey the Lord's prompting. First I sent a message asking if the telephone number was correct. "Yes," was the reply. Then, not knowing why, I sent a second message that contained the word "knowledge." I said something briefly about God's guidance in courtship and possible marriage. In the message I also added, "I feel prompted by God to send this message. I hope it makes sense."

My sister's friend responded that she could hardly believe the content of my text. It was something about which she had been intensely seeking God's will. The word "knowledge" assured her that God was listening to her prayers and would provide guidance for a possible life-shaping decision. By obeying the Holy Spirit, I had become a vehicle for God's answer to prayer. Her response to the word "knowledge" confirmed to me the importance of being keenly attentive to the Holy Spirit, as this chapter has urged.

Questions for Consideration

1. In what ways are we now proclaiming the gospel beyond our immediate congregation?
2. What will integrity in proclamation mean for our congregation?
3. What are the contexts that compose our area of ministry?
4. As individuals and as a congregation, are we listening to the Holy Spirit for guidance on what creative forms evangelism should take?
5. As a congregation, what are our resources for evangelism?

Additional Resources

Feucht, Sean. *Integrity: Character of the Kingdom*. New Kensington, PA: Whitaker House, 2016.

Johns, Mark D. *Our Context (Congregational Leader)*. Minneapolis: Augsburg Fortress, 2002.

Sherrard, Michael C. *Relational Apologetics: Defending the Christian Faith with Holiness, Respect, and Truth*. Grand Rapids: Kregel, 2015.

8
THE ETHICS OF EVANGELISM

Josh Sweeden, PhD

Indeed, this is our boast, the testimony of our conscience: we have behaved in the world with frankness and godly sincerity, not by earthly wisdom but by the grace of God—and all the more toward you.
—2 Corinthians 1:12, NRSV

Though my primary vocation is as a Christian minister and theological educator, I have spent a fair portion of my life working with my hands. Among my many life lessons, I have discovered there are right and wrong ways to use any tool. Improper use can cause danger to oneself or others. It can require extra time and energy and lead to poor quality work. Rarely have I learned how to use a tool by reading an instruction manual. Generally, I have learned proper use through apprenticeship and personal practice.

One memorable experience I had was as a teenager. It was a lesson in how to use a right-angle drill (the drill head is set at a ninety-degree angle to the handle). When used correctly, a right-angle drill is not a particularly dangerous tool. But I quickly learned there is also a wrong way to use one. My task was to bore holes through wall studs, easy enough. So I set to work, knowing very well that speed and efficiency were important to my boss. After a few successful efforts, I was confident I knew how to use the tool. So I continued in a sort of mindless rhythm, drilling holes around the room. Suddenly, on one stud, the drill bit stuck. Before I knew it my hand was violently pinned between the drill and a stud. I quickly realized what had happened: the bit had caught the edge of a knot in the wood. Because I wasn't maintaining proper pressure on the drill, it (rather than the bit) became the recipient of the motor's rotation.

The task of this chapter is to address the ethics of evangelism. Questions of ethics often revolve around right or wrong conduct. Much like using a right-angle drill, we could discuss proper and improper methods for evangelism. They are important. But in this chapter our interest is the relationship between ethics and evangelism. This topic must precede and govern method.

Unlike using a right-angle drill, evangelism is not a tool; it is a practice. We often tend to speak of evangelism as if it were a tool, but questions about how to properly use a drill are less *ethical* than simply *functional*. My hand was smashed, most would say, not because I was being unethical, but because I was foolish and inexperienced. Proper use of a tool is largely evaluated by satisfactory attention to its purpose; did it drill holes (function) as it was designed to do? While we may ask that of a tool, the primary question for evangelism is different: Are we practicing evangelism in a manner faithful to the gospel? Does our very practice announce the gospel? Those are questions of ethics, not of function or method.

THE CONTEXT OF OUR CONSIDERATION

The assumption of this chapter is that evangelism can never be anything less than ethical, just as Christian ethics can never be anything less than evangelistic. Evangelism is derived from the Greek word *euangelion*, meaning "good news." It points beyond the constructs of our world and toward the new reality in Christ, the new creation and the kingdom of God. Evangelism, then, in its very practice is the proclamation of good news and an invitation—a welcome and offering—to be a part of this new reality in Christ.

Ideally, we should not need to ask how evangelism can be ethical; evangelism is inherently ethical when it is truly good news.

Jesus not only proclaimed good news about the future but also proclaimed good news about the present. When he declared that "the kingdom of God has come near" (Mark 1:15, NIV; cf. Matt. 3:2) and healed the sick, raised the dead, and cast out demons, he was inaugurating the new creation in the midst of the old. Saying the "kingdom of God has come near" is another way of saying the kingdom of God is upon and among us (Luke 17:21). Jesus embodied and proclaimed the kingdom of God. He was the good news incarnate. In the same way, evangelism is *an act of the new creation*. Christians are proclaiming the good news that has entered the world through Jesus Christ (9:1-10).

Shortly after I was assigned to write this chapter, I shared my topic with a friend. He exclaimed, "Ethics and evangelism, what do they have to do with each other?" Since that conversation, I have become increasingly convinced his question reveals how many of us misunderstand evangelism. We generally assume ethics and evangelism are separate enterprises. Why is this so?

Perhaps for many, a distinction between ethics and evangelism derives from equating evangelism with technique or method. In this case evangelism is thought of as a task or activity used to accomplish a goal, such as increasing church attendance. As a result, ethics is a secondary consideration. The primary interest is evangelism's usefulness. Evangelism is not perceived as being opposed to ethics, of course, and there is agreement that it should be ethical. But fundamentally, evangelism is thought of as a tool for accomplishing some other end. A method can discredit the gospel, such as the rare practice of taking advantage of chronic hunger by giving bags of rice in exchange for conversions.

If evangelism is reduced to a technique or function evaluated by how successfully it produces professions of faith and more congregants, then utility or effectiveness will likely be valued above faithfulness to the kingdom of God and witness to the gospel.

For others, the distinction between ethics and evangelism is reinforced by their personal experience of evangelism. Their vision of evangelism is derivative of a "whatever works" approach. In this case, though, the result is a high degree of apprehension about evangelism that can even lead to its compartmentalization—a job for "professionals." This is unfortunate and disconcerting. Evangelism is not an optional practice for Christians. It is central to their calling as members of the body of Christ—as the church—who are to be witnesses of the good news found in Jesus Christ. In my own ministry experiences, I have seen these two perspectives inadvertently perpetuate the false distinction between evangelism and ethics. In part, the perspectives reflect differences in theology. The way one understands salvation, the church, and the culmination of all creation has much to do with how evangelism is conceived and practiced. But one's context also plays a major role. Whether that is a passion to mitigate the decline of church membership or turn the tide of post-Christendom (a reality in Western culture in which the church's long-held social, political, and cultural power is abating) or, as in the case of some, a reluctance to engage the "E-word" altogether.[1] I have seen the harm both perspectives can cause. Without any substantive vision of faithful evangelism, evangelistic practice simply reflects the church's cultural and contextual pressures. Such evangelism struggles to embody good news, because the good news always points beyond ourselves and our limited perspectives of the world toward new life and hope in Christ.

PRACTICE OF EVANGELISM

To move beyond the unfortunate distinction between evangelism and ethics, Christians must recover evangelism as *a practice*. A practice differs from a procedure, technique, or method because its purpose is not derived from its *use value*—that is, the degree to which it is determined to be *useful*. Emblematic of this kind of utilitarian thinking is the notion that the "ends justify the means." This common idiom presupposes the "means" are best weighed by their ability to achieve some "end." The means matter only in their ability to accomplish a desired goal. Taken to the extreme, the phrase can be used to justify destruction or dishonesty in the name of progress. Most people use the phrase without thinking of its presuppositions, but it does illustrate the challenges of faithful evangelism in today's context. Recovering evangelism as a *practice* counters an "ends justify the means" mentality. This might seem like a strange way of thinking in our utilitarian world, where value is often equated with usefulness.

Our contemporary context makes it challenging to think of ethics and evangelism. Nevertheless, evangelism must always be faithful to and express the gospel of Jesus Christ. The practice of evangelism must embody the end itself—namely, the new creation in Christ Jesus and the very character of God's kingdom. Philosopher Alasdair MacIntyre can help here. He explains that practices are defined by the internal goods they "realize" in trying to perform the practices with excellence.[2] Brad Kallenberg is also helpful. He uses playing chess as an example:

> I can bribe my son with pieces of candy to learn the game of chess. But at some point he may begin to enjoy the game of chess for itself. At this point he has become a practitioner and member of the greater community of chess players. He has, furthermore, become hooked on its internal reward—the joy of chess.[3]

Take another example. Years ago in Kansas City I saw billboards advertising the Kansas City Royals. The Royals were having a terrible season. Attendance was in sharp decline. The billboards used the phrase "For the Love of the Game." The Royals were banking on fans loving the game itself, not on whether the Royals were winning or losing.

Similarly, evangelism has an internal kingdom value that must be expressed in its practice. Just as the internal good or value of playing chess is the joy of chess, the internal good or value of evangelism is the announcement of the reign of God, actualizing the good news, not its external success or failure.

The practice of evangelism must embody the good news it proclaims. It must reflect the reign of God and announce the hope Christ offers our broken world. Less than this would be unethical. Evangelism is good news when it tells others of the peace, compassion, hospitality, and self-giving love of Jesus Christ. Evangelism is an ethic because its very practice is consistent with the reign of God to which the church bears witness.

Let's consider three lenses through which to evaluate our practice of evangelism. *First*, evangelism offers *shalom*, the peace of God. It is a practice of reconciliation and restoration in the world. Evangelistic practices participate in the transformation of the world through love rather than hate, charity rather than divisiveness, and through grace that frees instead of guilt that enslaves. *Second*, evangelism truly welcomes the other. Rather than setting preconditions on those whom God is drawing near or instead of issuing condemnation, evangelism announces a word and world of mercy by inviting others to experience full fellowship with God. An evangelizing community of Christ opens itself to the gifts of *the other* by seeing Christ in the stranger and by considering how, through that person, Christ might desire transformation for the Christian community itself. *Third*, evangelism exhibits the upside-down kingdom of God. It counters the powers and principalities of the world by embodying Christ's way of self-emptying, sacrificial love. Such evangelism gives attention to the margins and forgotten places of persons and society. It seeks healing where there is brokenness. It testifies to an upside-down new reality in which the least are the greatest (Luke 22:26).

WESLEYAN IMPLICATIONS FOR PROCLAIMING THE GOOD NEWS

Practiced faithfully, evangelism bears witness to the in-breaking reign of God. The proclamation of the good news is the act of making Christ known. It includes verbal and written testimony. But we also evangelize—make Christ known—by our lives, individually and corporately. Proclamation includes invitation through the compelling beauty of the gospel, which calls everyone ever so intently, "Come and see" (John 1:39, KJV).

The Wesleyan-Holiness tradition is committed to explicit evangelism. But it also emphasizes the ways evangelism and ethics are inseparable. Indeed, from a Wesleyan perspective it is appropriate to state that our ethics is our evangelism, inasmuch as our evangelism is our ethics.

This was evident in the ministry of John Wesley, his hopes and expectations for the Methodists, and the practices of subsequent Wesleyan generations. For example, Wesley coupled evangelism with fervor for social reform. The conjunction of evangelism and social reform is visible in Wesley's emphasis on sanctification. He believed sanctification of one's life by God's grace entails increasing love not only for God but also for one's neighbor.

A Christian's whole person is being transformed toward deeper and "constant communion" with God. Wesley was adamant that Christians were called to holiness of heart *and* life and that holiness must also be translated into good news in concrete and tangible ways. In one of his sermons Wesley asked, "Why has Christianity done so little good in the world?"[4] The failure happens, Wesley answered, because Christians have not adequately evidenced the reign of God in themselves and in the broader society. Evangelism, Wesley insisted, should be inseparable from how we live in the world.

In the Wesleyan tradition, evangelism is also thought of as a natural outflow of practicing the means of grace. The means of grace include the following: (1) "works of piety" (e.g., prayer, fasting, and participating in the sacraments) and (2) "works of mercy" (e.g., visiting the sick and imprisoned, giving generously, addressing needs of the poor). Wesley called them "ordinary channels whereby [God] might convey to men [and women], preventing, justifying, and sanctifying grace."[5] When practiced consistently, the means of grace deepen one's love for God and for one's neighbor. They help Christians extend God's grace to others and proclaim the good news. In this way, they enable all Christians to be evangelists.

Let's discuss visiting the sick, one "work of mercy," as an example of the practice of evangelism. This work of mercy Wesley highly regarded.[6] Visiting the sick has biblical and historical foundations (Matt. 25:31-36). Jesus modeled and commanded care for the sick (Mark 1:32-34; 2:1-12; Luke 4:38-44). Obedient to Jesus, the early church embraced the practice as core to its identity and witness. Sociologist Rodney Stark highlights the contribution that care for the sick—especially for women—made to the church's growth during its first three centuries. During epidemics and disasters, the church opened its doors to the sick and dying. Merciful Christian aid resulted in the conversion of many. Stark also notes that the church's care for women increased fertility rates. This contributed to the generational increase of Christians.[7]

Visiting the sick remains an embodiment of the good news. I recently heard a seminary graduate who is a chaplain in a rescue mission tell of his journey to faith. It began with his mother, who encountered the love of Christ while in a hospital. She was being treated for a nonmalignant brain tumor. The parents had no church community or commitment of faith. But a family friend in a nearby town had been praying for the mother.

After she was admitted to the hospital, the friend contacted her pastor, who then called the pastor of the local Church of the Nazarene. Church members began to visit the mother. The selfless care they offered was a concrete expression of God's love. It provided a compelling invitation to the parents to "come and see."

My faith journey is similar. My mother grew up in an abusive, dysfunctional home, which she escaped during her senior year of high school. The pastor's family in the local Church of the Nazarene took her in and gave her a home. They offered healing amid her brokenness. They gave her a vision of a new life and helped her go to college. My mother then devoted her life to serving others, just as the pastor's family had done for her. When I think of my mother's story, I am aware I am a recipient of the Wesleyan impetus to visit the sick. John Wesley correctly expanded the meaning of illness: "By the sick, I do not mean only those that keep their bed, or that are sick in the strictest sense. Rather I would include all such as are in a state of affliction, whether of mind or body; and that whether they are good or bad, whether they fear God or not."[8]

My mother was loved while "in a state of affliction." Through love and care she experienced the commonwealth of God—a concrete expression of the good news that overcomes this world's bad news. By the Christian love shown to my mother, she was invited into the world of the Beatitudes (Matt. 5:3-12). Jesus's "blessedness" offered an alternative to the violence and scarcity she had known as a child.

The chaplain's story and my mother's story remind me that faithfully visiting the sick is an act of the new creation. In each instance there was proclamation of good news; in each instance there was an invitation. It is striking, too, that visiting the sick is not a technique or tool. Instead, it is a work of mercy in which Christians point to the in-breaking reign of God in which the sick are healed and the imprisoned set free. Visiting the sick is a profound way of practicing evangelism.

ON EARTH AS IT IS IN HEAVEN

What has ethics to do with evangelism? How may we evangelize ethically? These are key questions in today's context. The problem is that the questions assume evangelism and ethics are separable. If that happens, evangelism is too easily understood as a means to an end (i.e., using a right-angle drill) whose purpose is functional rather than fundamental. The questions also assume we can do a lot on our own, by proper use of a "tool." John Wesley was keen to remind Christians that our response to God is always grace empowered; it is God who calls, saves, and sustains. Our task is to testify to Christ and the new creation he provides. Therefore, Christians are called to be bearers of the good news in Christ, knowing there is power enough in that news (Rom. 1:16).

As Christians we would do well to assert and practice ethics and evangelism as inseparable; our practice must embody the good news itself. The way we are called to live in the world as heralds of the new creation in Christ should always precede and govern questions of method or technique (Phil. 1:27).

Moreover, there is inherent value in the proclamation of good news, no matter its immediate outcome. This is the confidence we have in Christ, the power of the gospel, and the Holy Spirit's faithfulness. It enables us to confidently pray the Lord's Prayer, "Thy kingdom come, Thy will be done" (Matt. 6:10, KJV), because we believe God's *euangelion* is now breaking in on earth, even as it is in heaven. When we live this prayer, we extend its beauty to others and offer a powerful invitation grounded in the ethic of God's kingdom.

Questions for Consideration

1. Consider various ways the good news is proclaimed (spoken, enacted, etc.) in the Scriptures. How might that variety inform possibilities for evangelism today?
2. Is evangelism sometimes compartmentalized in your Christian community? How can it be better acknowledged as part of your church's ongoing practices and life together?
3. What personal or corporate Christian practices do you regularly engage in that you had not thought of as evangelistic practices?
4. Beyond evangelism, how prevalent is utilitarianism in other Christian practices? What ways can those practices take on more of an "in earth, as it is in heaven" (Matt. 6:10, KJV) perspective?

Additional Resources

Graham, Elaine. *Apologetics without Apology: Speaking of God in a World Troubled by Religion*. Eugene, OR: Cascade Books, 2017.

Heath, Elaine A. *The Mystic Way of Evangelism: A Contemplative Vision for Christian Outreach*. 2nd ed. Grand Rapids: Baker Academic, 2017.

Kallenberg, Brad J. *Live to Tell: Evangelism for a Postmodern Age*. Grand Rapids: Brazos Press, 2002.

Knight, Henry H., III, and F. Douglas Powe Jr. *Transforming Evangelism: The Wesleyan Way of Sharing Faith*. Nashville: Discipleship Resources, 2006.

Stone, Bryan P. *Evangelism after Pluralism: The Ethics of Christian Witness*. Grand Rapids: Baker Academic, 2018.

9

THE HOLY SPIRIT'S FREEDOM TO CRAFT CONVERSION

Grant Zweigle, DMin

The wind blows wherever it pleases. You hear its sound, but you cannot tell where it comes from or where it is going. So it is with everyone born of the Spirit.
—John 3:8, NIV

Have you ever been surprised by the Christian conversion of a friend, relative, coworker, or casual acquaintance? Bruce's conversion surprised me. Bruce was a former Marine who lived near the VA Hospital located around the corner from our urban neighborhood church on Beacon Hill, Seattle. After my first Sunday as pastor of the church, Bruce cornered me and invited himself to lunch with my family. That was the beginning of a beautifully strange pastoral relationship.

Bruce made it clear he was not interested in spiritual things. After one sermon he said to me, "Pastor, when you are up there preaching, I don't understand a word you are saying." On another occasion he explained how his father taught him that when you die, you are put in a box, and that is the end of it.

It seemed Bruce attended church primarily for the possibility of an invitation to lunch and the hope of pastoral visits to his ramshackle house off of Martin Luther King Jr. Boulevard. Bruce frequently left messages asking me to stop by and visit him, usually with an agenda in mind, such as picking an apple from the tree in his front yard or taking out his trash. As an earnest young pastor, I attempted to engage him in spiritual conversations on these visits, but Bruce always had a way of redirecting the conversation to his own ends.

I was trained in practices of evangelism, sometimes referred to as "encounter evangelism." These methods included special evangelistic services, personal evangelism, event evangelism, and friendship evangelism. Conversion in response to a prepared presentation of the gospel, combined with an urgent appeal to accept Jesus Christ as Savior and Lord, was the goal.[1] The method was designed to lead people in a "sinner's prayer." They would be encouraged to attend church, read the Bible, pray, and share their faith with others. This was our desire for Bruce.

So we conducted revival services. During one of these the guest speaker made an evangelistic appeal at the end of his sermon. Much to my surprise, Bruce responded to the invitation. This was the first time I saw Bruce at the altar. My heart leaped with joy at the thought of his conversion. I knelt across from Bruce and asked him what had prompted him to come to the altar. His response confounded me. "I like the way the preacher did *this*," Bruce explained while gesturing upwards and outwards with his arms. That was all I could get out of him.

One of our members, Ms. Adrian, was trained in personal evangelism. She used pieces of colored string to present the gospel to children. Ms. Adrian cared deeply for Bruce and was lovingly concerned about the condition of his soul. She presented the gospel to him on numerous occasions. But he was impervious to her efforts. Bruce seemed immune to all our evangelistic strategies. Our hopes and prayers for his sudden conversion went unfulfilled.

So I was surprised five years later to be standing beside Bruce as he sat in his wheelchair next to Lake Washington, waiting to be baptized. Ms. Adrian stood beside him, holding his hand. As a breeze passed through Bruce's thinning gray hair, he affirmed each of the baptismal questions: "Will you be baptized in the faith as expressed in the Apostles' Creed?" *I will.* "Do you acknowledge Jesus Christ as your personal Savior, and do you realize that He saves you now?" *I do.* "Will you obey God's holy will and keep his commandments, walking in them all the days of your life?" *I will.* "Bruce MacMeekin, I baptize you in the name of the Father, and of the Son, and of the Holy Spirit. Amen."[2]

Yes, I was surprised by Bruce's conversion. Most of my attempts to engage Bruce in spiritual conversations had failed. The revival service had yielded an odd result. The frequent gospel presentations seemed to land on deaf ears. Bruce was "poor in spirit" (Matt. 5:3, KJV). But the kingdom of God was open to him! The Spirit was blowing through his life in ways imperceptible to our eyes.

Perhaps, as a pastor in the Wesleyan theological tradition, I shouldn't have been surprised by Bruce's conversion. Perhaps my reliance on more traditional evangelism techniques had kept me from seeing how the Sprit was already working in his life. Perhaps I needed a firmer Wesleyan foundation for my evangelistic practices!

CONVERSION AND THE HOLY SPIRIT

Howard Snyder reminds us that John Wesley's understanding of what God is up to in the world is "audaciously optimistic."[3] He writes, "Wesleyan theology is saturated with hope, expectancy, optimism of grace and the grace of optimism. This hope is based not on human intelligence or technology but on Jesus' resurrection, God's promise, and the present work of the Spirit."[4]

Christians in the Wesleyan tradition place special emphasis on the necessity and possibility of conversion. John Wesley famously charged his preachers to "save as many souls as you can," emphasizing the urgency of their evangelistic ministry.[5] But it would be a misreading of Wesley to think he was urging his preachers to put their hope in human intelligence, persuasion, and carefully crafted gospel presentations to secure conversions.

Critics of early Methodism described conversion in the Wesleyan movement as resulting from "manipulation, chicanery, emotional conditioning, and the like."[6] But that is not how John Wesley saw it! Wesleyan theologian William Abraham reminds us that for Wesley, "to be born again, to receive the witness of the Holy Spirit, to be justified, to be sanctified, and the like, was to be subject to divine action . . . *divine* [*action*] *brought about by the Holy Spirit*."[7]

While few in the Wesleyan theological tradition would disagree with Wesley's emphasis on the action of the Holy Spirit in bringing about conversion, the evangelistic practices of some of Wesley's theological heirs often reveal a dependency on human action that might suggest the converting work of the Spirit can be accomplished by human planning and techniques. Looking back, I can see how some of my early evangelistic efforts could be characterized as manipulative and overly reliant on an emotional conditioning of the prospect.

In his book *Transforming Conversion*, Gordon Smith affirms the revivalist heritage for its stress on the necessity and possibility of conversion. He appreciates its emphasis on the need for people "to take personal responsibility for their lives and for their response to the claims of the gospel."[8] However, he warns against any practice that might diminish the Spirit's freedom to achieve a person's conversion in whatever way the Spirit chooses. Some Christians, Smith observes, "have been taught simple formulas in a one-size-fits-all approach to evangelism: ask the right questions, lead people through a series of simple statements, guide them through a timely prayer, and one can state with confidence that these persons have become Christian believers."[9] Such practices may lack sensitivity to the Holy Spirit. As a corrective, Smith reminds us, "Evangelism involves discerning the work of the Spirit, learning how to be attentive to how the Spirit is at work in this person at this time and in this place."[10]

EVANGELISM WITH AN END IN MIND

An examination of Wesley's own evangelistic practices reveals patience and attention to the work of the Spirit in those who joined the early Methodist communities. In his exploration of John Wesley's evangelistic practices, Ron Benefiel describes Wesley as a passionate evangelist who expected his Methodist preachers to focus on preaching the gospel and saving souls.[11] Wesley was intentional about bringing the gospel to the people. Methodist field preaching was "a movement out of the cathedral and into the marketplace, and out of established sacred spaces into unconventional public squares. In essence, field preaching was an exercise in meeting people on their home turf."[12]

However, it was not primarily in the field but in Methodism's small groups that people experienced conversion and assurance of forgiveness.[13] Wesley was concerned, not simply about a person's immediate response to an evangelistic appeal, but with renewal of the human heart and transformation of the whole person. "For Wesley," concludes Benefiel, "the mission of evangelism was not limited to calling people to forgiveness but extended to calling them to Christian perfection. Field preaching, class meetings and bands all worked together as part of Wesley's overall strategy of evangelism."[14]

Wesley's focus on renewal of the heart and transformation of the whole person as the goal of evangelism should encourage us to take a longer view of the Spirit's work. It should remind us not to become frustrated by the apparently slow conversion of persons for whom we are praying. Consequently, Scott Jones defines evangelism as "that set of loving, intentional activities governed by the goal of initiating persons into Christian discipleship in response to the reign of God."[15] Evangelism often takes a long time and involves periods of questioning, wrestling, exploring, testing, and experiencing the practices and beliefs of a Christian community before commitments are made.[16]

This perspective on evangelism was confirmed during my years as pastor in Vancouver, Canada. I became more attentive to the work of the Spirit in transforming people and less anxious about immediately securing their conversion.

Vancouver is a challenging place to minister. In addition to having one of the lowest rates of church participation in North America, attempts to secure a person's conversion from one religion or belief system to another are viewed negatively. Proselytism of any kind is antithetical to Canadian multicultural values. As a result, many of the Spirit-filled Christians in my congregation were reluctant to engage in any form of evangelism they viewed as inconsistent with those values.

And yet, during my years of ministry in Vancouver, we saw the conversion of sinners and the transformation of people's lives. Conversions happened; the lost were found. But conversions rarely happened during revival services or after carefully prepared presentations of the gospel. More often they occurred during the longer spiritual journey of someone who had a friend or relative in our congregation. Conversions happened because of loving, intentional investments by Christian friends, family, and pastors.

EVANGELISM THAT IS PERSONAL

We practiced evangelism that is personal—that is, practices attentive to the work of the Holy Spirit in the lives of friends, relatives, coworkers, and acquaintances. Evangelism that is personal is practiced by people willing to take the long and patient journey toward renewal in the image of God. Such practices included prayer, sharing personal stories, and going on personal journeys with people.[17]

Australian evangelist John Dickson calls prayer "the hidden mission" of evangelism.[18] Prayer reminds us that human transformation is first and finally the work of the Spirit, not ours. Evangelism requires "faith more than activism, dependence more than programs and humility more than boldness."[19]

In our Vancouver congregation this included regular gatherings to pray for the Spirit to open the hearts of friends, family, coworkers, and acquaintances. Congregants were taught the "high-five" prayer, keeping the names of five people on a regular prayer list. These names included the children of the church, forgetters, and outsiders. Through prayer we released control of outcomes and confessed our dependence on the Holy Spirit to call, convict, and convert those for whom we were praying.

Rather than relying on planned gospel presentations with predetermined scripts and results, we encouraged a studied immersion in the story of God as recorded in Scripture, the story of Jesus in the Gospels, and familiarity with apostolic preaching in Acts and the Epistles. By becoming familiar with the grand salvation themes of the Bible, through regular study and rehearsal of the Gospel narratives and apostolic preaching, congregants became prepared to give an account of the hope they had in Jesus Christ (1 Pet. 3:15).

We encouraged people to write and reflect on their personal story, how they came to know and follow Jesus. One exercise involved writing a life timeline and identifying significant moments of spiritual insight and turning toward Jesus. Significant people who helped congregants grow in their knowledge and experience of God were identified. Not everyone's experience conformed to a well-defined narrative of "before I met Jesus," "how I met Jesus," "after I met Jesus." More often a person's journey involved a few steps forward in understanding, a few steps back, and moments of significant interest followed by periods of neglect. But as people reflected on their journeys, they were often able to see how the Spirit had worked over the whole course of their lives. This helped them become attentive to the Spirit's activity in other people.

Being attentive to the Spirit's activity in a person requires being willing to take what is often a long journey toward Christian faith. A lifelong member of our church named John took the long journey with Ken, his unchurched neighbor. Without pressure, but with loving intention, John made friendly inquiries into Ken's life, invited him to church activities, shared parts of his own spiritual journey with Ken, and offered to pray with him when it seemed appropriate. Twenty-three years after becoming neighbors Ken made a profession of faith and began following Jesus. Ken now walks with others on their journey to Jesus, attentive to the work of the Spirit in the lives of his neighbors and friends.

Amie lived next door to Isabelle and went to school with Isabelle's children. As Isabelle aged, Amie offered to drive her to church. After several months of sitting in the parking lot while Isabelle attended the worship service, Amie slipped into the back of the sanctuary. She was surprised by how welcoming and hospitable the people were. She returned and began making friends. Dawn included Amie in service opportunities through the church. Kadee and Amie built a friendship over coffee and social visits. During these visits Kadee shared her personal story of how she came to know, love, and follow Jesus. During one of these visits, Kadee asked Amie if she would like to know what it means to follow Jesus. Amie expressed interest, and they began studying the Gospel of John, where she learned more about Jesus's story. Within a few years, Amie was baptized and is now a regular participant in the life and mission of the church. She is growing in love for God and others, which is evident in her compassionate service to others.

REIMAGINING CONVERSION: THE PORCH, THE DOOR, AND THE HOUSE

One way John Wesley described the journey toward conversion utilizes the image of a house with three main parts: the porch of repentance, the door of faith, and the house of holiness.[20] This image resists a rigid order of salvation while retaining an emphasis on the work of the Spirit to produce decisive evangelical faith. In this picture, the end toward which the Christian journey moves, and therefore the ultimate goal of evangelism, is our renewal in the image of God so that all of our relationships are characterized by love.[21] Evangelistic practices such as personal prayer, sharing personal stories, and going on personal journeys with people are aimed toward that end. As a maturing pastor, I was influenced in my evangelistic practices by Wesley's image of the house as descriptive of the spiritual journey.[22]

I first met Enoch in the parking lot of our church, where he dropped off his mom for worship services and other activities. Enoch's parents immigrated to Vancouver from Southeast Asia when he was a boy. His parents struggled to make ends meet, and an illness in his family made life difficult. His parents' faith was strong, but Enoch showed little interest in spiritual things. In high school he was attracted to Vancouver's drug and gang culture. In college he supplied drugs to classmates. But when his friends began engaging in criminal activity that put others at risk, Enoch began to have second thoughts about how he was living.

Enoch's mom was praying for her son and asked us to pray as well. When she heard we were offering an Alpha course, a ten-week introduction to the Christian faith, she encouraged her son to attend. Alpha is an evangelistic program intentionally designed to provide a safe and hospitable place for people to explore the Christian faith. While appeals are made throughout the course for people to consider trusting Jesus as Lord and Savior, conversion is not a requirement for participation.

For Enoch, the Alpha format, which included a meal, a video, and dessert fellowship, allowed space to begin making a few friends at our church. It provided a place to ask questions as he tried to make sense of his life. Enoch saw the transformation occurring in his mom's life through her participation in the life and mission of our church. That inspired him to participate in our congregation. The people he met were authentic, open, and hospitable, a stark contrast to his gang friends.

Enoch heard about a Christian nonprofit organization our church supported in Vancouver's downtown eastside. He began volunteering, serving meals to the homeless. He was a student at the Emily Carr art school in Vancouver and offered to teach art to the people he served. When we learned about Enoch's artistic talents, our young adults started a worship arts team and invited Enoch to participate. The worship arts team studied a passage of Scripture from the lectionary and created artistic pieces related to that passage. Through this activity Enoch began reading and studying the Scriptures, learning the grand story of salvation in the Bible and reflecting on the good news of the gospel of Jesus Christ.

Looking back on that time, Enoch told me he appreciated the space he was given to explore Christianity and the church. He said that if there had been any "high pressure sales techniques," he would not have stayed around. Enoch began to pray. When he recalled things in his life that did not show love for God or others, he asked forgiveness. The stress of exiting his previous lifestyle was intense. His most common prayer was, "Lord, I've dug myself in a huge hole—get me out of here!" Enoch was stepping onto the porch of repentance.

Enoch's attendance at our Sunday worship services became consistent, and his involvement in the life and mission of our local church increased. When he was asked to help with the elementary-aged boys Sunday school class, he thought to himself, "If I'm going to teach these boys, I need to get my life together!" Around this time Enoch noticed his new life in Christ beginning to "stick." He doesn't remember a specific moment of sudden conversion, but through the loving influence of his new Christian friends, he passed from the porch of repentance through the door of faith.

Enoch found work with the Christian nonprofit and also took a short-term mission trip with our church. These experiences opened his heart to hopeless and hurting people and deepened his desire for change. But some of his old habits were hard to break. When he violated the trust of his employer, he was fired. This was a difficult point in his life and a sign that he needed to walk in the light and leave his deeds of darkness behind. I remember meeting with Enoch during this season of his life. Over bowls of hot Vietnamese beef-noodle soup and cups of coffee, we talked about what it means to surrender our lives completely to the Holy Spirit. Enoch was moving from the door of faith into the house of holy love.

Today Enoch is a missionary with the Church of the Nazarene, serving on the Asia-Pacific Region. In addition to his work as a photojournalist and graphic artist with World Mission Communications in Manila, Philippines, he also teaches art to children, youth, and adults in some of Manila's most notorious slums. Enoch practices evangelism just as he was evangelized: he prays for the people he is teaching; he uses art as a means of sharing the story of God and the good news of the gospel; and he patiently journeys with people as they move more fully into the house of God's holy love.

Enoch's conversion was neither sudden nor dramatic. But the Spirit was blowing through Enoch's life. Our church was patient and attentive to God's work in his life. Not content with simply leading Enoch through a "sinner's prayer" or attempting to get him "to the altar," his Christian friends focused on the renewal of Enoch's life in the image of God so that all his relationships could be characterized by Christian love. This was not the work of one person, but evangelism by the whole church in cooperation with the Holy Spirit.

CONCLUSION

In his book *Evangelism after Christendom*, Bryan Stone suggests that "the very possibility of Christian evangelism . . . is premised wholly upon the faithfulness of the Spirit's witness in our lives rather than in our own ability to calculate and predict how our obedience might translate into effectiveness."[23] As the church continues to move into the twenty-first century, an increased awareness of and dependence on the faithful presence of the Holy Spirit in our lives and congregations is the key to our evangelistic practices.

Our evangelistic techniques, plans, and programs are insufficient by themselves to bring about the renewal of men and women Wesley envisioned and the Scriptures promise. But if we practice evangelism in a way that is attentive to the Holy Spirit, infused with prayer, informed by Scripture, and intentionally present with the people we love and desire to see transformed, we might be happily surprised by conversion. Let us always be confident that the Spirit is working in the world around us.

Questions for Consideration

1. Have you ever been surprised by the Christian conversion of a friend, relative, coworker, or casual acquaintance? What surprised you?
2. How do you stay attentive to the work of the Holy Spirit in the lives of people around you?
3. What are some of the strengths of revivalist evangelistic methods? What are some of the weaknesses of revivalist evangelistic methods?
4. Reflect on your whole spiritual journey. Who are some of the key people who helped you grow in love for God and others? How did they help you?
5. Write the names of five people who are not currently following Jesus. Ask the Holy Spirit to renew the hearts of these five. What step could you take this week to connect with one of the people you named?

Additional Resources

Clapper, Gregory S. *As If the Heart Mattered: A Wesleyan Spirituality*. Eugene, OR: Wipf and Stock, 2014.

Dickson, John. *The Best Kept Secret of Christian Mission: Promoting the Gospel with More Than Our Lips*. Grand Rapids: Zondervan, 2010.

Jones, Scott J. *The Evangelistic Love of God and Neighbor: A Theology of Witness and Discipleship*. Nashville: Abingdon Press, 2003.

Smith, Gordon T. *Transforming Conversion: Rethinking the Language and Contours of Christian Initiation*. Grand Rapids: Baker Academic, 2010.

Stone, Bryan P. *Evangelism after Christendom: The Theology and Practice of Christian Witness*. Grand Rapids: Brazos Press, 2007.

Zweigle, Grant. *Worship, Wonder, and Way: Reimagining Evangelism as Missional Practice*. Kansas City: Beacon Hill Press of Kansas City, 2015.

10

EVANGELIZING TOWARD DISCIPLESHIP

WORSHIP, SACRAMENTS, THE MEANS OF GRACE, AND EVANGELISM

T. Scott Daniels, PhD

All who desire the grace of God are to wait for it in the means he hath ordained.
—John Wesley

Jessica walked into my office at the university with tears streaming down her cheeks. Through her sobs she asked, "When do you know you've become an Anglican?"

"What happened?" I asked.

"I think I've become addicted to liturgy," she replied.

A few weeks beforehand, I had given my theology and ministry course a worship assignment. They were to visit two different worship services—

one from a "high" liturgical tradition and another from a "low" liturgical tradition—and reflect in writing on what they observed about the formative nature of each. The assignment did not ask students to reflect on whether they liked the service or if it fit their particular taste. In fact, I told them the only way to fail was to tell me if they "liked or disliked" any aspect of the service. The primary question I asked was, "If you attended this church for ten years, how would the worship of the church have changed you?" In other words, I wanted them to discern what the various practices of the church were trying to achieve.

Jessica and some of her friends in the course had chosen for their high liturgical worship service a lovely Anglican church within walking distance of the campus. Although most of her friends found the service odd and foreign compared to how they had worshipped in their home churches, something about the rhythms and practices of the Anglican liturgy resonated with Jessica. She began returning for worship not only for Sunday services but also for daily morning prayers.

A morning-prayer service led to her tears in my office and to her minor existential worship crisis. That morning the weather had been brutally cold and the roads quite icy. She bundled up and walked into the Anglican sanctuary only to discover she and the priest were the only congregants who had braved the elements. Despite the initial awkwardness, she and the priest proceeded through the liturgy. As she sat in my office recounting her worship experience that morning, she asked, "Do you know what one of the four daily office texts for today was? 'For where two or three are gathered in my name, I am there among them' [Matt. 18:20, NRSV]!" She recounted that when she and the priest reached that Gospel reading, they looked at each other and began to cry. By the time she reached my office, the tears hadn't ceased.

As I probed for more of what she was experiencing, Jessica shared not only how new and beautiful all of the liturgy was but also the transformation taking place as she participated in the prayers of the people, as she regularly came to the Lord's Table, and as she heard repeatedly the full breadth of Scripture. The abundance of Scripture readings had been especially important. In fact, Jessica's statement was, "I think I hear more Scripture in one morning-prayer service than I hear in a year of attending worship at my home church."

That meeting with Jessica took place twenty years ago. But I've had dozens of similar conversations with students since then. What I, and many others, have sensed in Christians—young and old—is not rejection of the spontaneity and personal passion of many "low" liturgical church services, but a hunger for connection, for being rooted in something that transcends the momentary. They hunger for practices that in their rhythm and meaning form deeper habits of faithfulness and holiness than they've often experienced in more contemporary forms of worship.

My hope in this chapter is not to convince or convert those raised in low liturgical traditions to join Jessica in Anglican morning prayers, or even to argue that a return to earlier liturgical forms might aid in church growth. My purpose is to recognize—for the entire body of Christ—the wealth of wisdom related to Christian formation and spiritual transformation given to us in and through the "means of grace" as practiced by the church throughout Christian history. There are formational and, equally important, evangelistic opportunities and habits missing from many contemporary churches; too often several of the historic means of grace have been set aside.

WESLEY AND THE MEANS OF GRACE

John Wesley ministered when the forms and practices of ministry were beginning to come under intense critique. Amid the revivals and renewal movements of the eighteenth century in Europe and North America, leaders with an "evangelical" zeal became much more interested in the inner change of heart accomplished by the Holy Spirit than in the rigid formalism of various state-church traditions. John Wesley, with his passion for people experiencing and living out a life of warmhearted holiness, should be counted among them. He, too, was suspicious of the formalism often associated with the sacraments and practices of the Anglican Church of his day.

However, when one reads Wesley's sermons, letters, and other reflections on the various "means of grace," one finds him caught in something of a conundrum. On the one hand, he openly rejects the coldness of religious formalism. In the opening of his sermon "The Means of Grace," Wesley decries the cooling of Christlike love in some believers. They were beginning "to mistake the *means* for the *end*, and to place religion . . .

in doing those outward works, [rather] than in a heart renewed after the image of God."[1] Wesley seems to be empathetic toward those who have rejected empty participation in practices of the faith when there appears to be no true transformation of the heart in love flowing from them.

However, on the other hand, Wesley sees the rejection of those practices—in particular prayer (public and private), searching the Scriptures (alone in study and in a congregation through preaching and teaching), receiving the Lord's Supper, and the administration of baptism—as failing to obey God's clear command. Such failures miss opportunities for God's Spirit to continue transforming believers. For Wesley, by participating in these "outward signs, words, or actions" one opens oneself to the "preventing, justifying, or sanctifying grace"[2] of God. Wesley says, "I do expect that [God] will fulfil his word, that he will meet and bless me in this way. Yet not for the sake of any works which I have done, nor for the merit of my righteousness; but merely through the merits, and sufferings, and love of his Son, in whom he is always well pleased."[3]

To put it more plainly, while Wesley was suspicious of and rejected formal religion that failed to bring about inner transformation, he nevertheless thought of no better methods (he was a "Method-ist" after all) than the historic sacraments and practices—rightly used—for receiving and experiencing the transforming activity of God's grace.

Those of us raised in the more spontaneous worship of the typical evangelical church need to pay attention to the opportunities for formation and evangelization we are missing because of either neglect or absence of these more historic means of grace. Beyond that, we must also recognize that the forms of worship practiced in lower church traditions are also powerfully formative. The question is, Are they forming (or counter-forming) people in ways consistent with the kingdom of God?

Here are two examples of what I mean.

First, when I send students to visit worship services and instruct them to ask themselves, "How is the liturgy meant to be formative?" their responses almost always reframe their thinking. They are accustomed to asking themselves, "Did I like it?" I don't think that happens only because they have been raised in a consumer-driven culture. That is an important factor. They also ask, "Do I like it?" because that is how worship has been directed. As one who regularly plans worship, I confess that most weeks the question that drives planning is, "Will the congregation enjoy what we are doing today?" instead of, "Will God be glorified in what is said, done, and sung today?" Similarly, worship and sermon are shaped by a concern to be "relevant," to meet people "where they are," rather than discerning where the gospel of Jesus should take us. In other words, we shouldn't be surprised or hurt when people treat coming to church "critically"—the way a film critic treats going to the theater. We foster that attitude by forming worship first and foremost as driven by the "tastes of the consumers of worship" we have helped form.

A *second* example of inadvertent formation in typical evangelical forms of worship is creating celebrity-pastor–driven ministries—namely, "cults of personality." Lower liturgical services tend to trade traditional *liturgy* (the "work of the people") that includes the whole congregation for the activity of a handful of people. Usually this includes a worship leader and a preacher. Although the centrality of the sermon can be a beautiful thing in typical evangelical worship, because it too often becomes the central part of worship, there is tremendous pressure on the one preaching to achieve significant transformation week after week. By contrast, in a traditional liturgical service, where the high point and culmination of worship is gathering at the Lord's Table and where the homily lasts ten to fifteen minutes (usually in the middle of the service), congregations can endure a few less-than-riveting sermons. But in lower church worship, where the high point is a sermon lasting thirty to forty-five minutes, it often seems the entire weight of worship falls on the significance of the proclaimed Word.

Along with Wesley, I affirm that a primary means of grace and means of evangelism is studying Scripture through preaching. But if that important means of grace is not richly supplemented by additional means of grace, it receives disproportionate attention that can become counterproductive. When this happens, we should not be surprised when we evangelicals form people who move from church to church, chasing new, exciting, and "relevant teaching." That is primarily how they have been formed. And we should not be surprised to find we have created a culture of "celebrity pastors" who build large movements that often collapse when the "celebrity" fails personally or morally. This can happen because of the pressure imposed on them by their congregants.

So how may we develop a balanced approach that more completely serves evangelism and discipleship? How may all the means of grace be employed to form believers while also serving to invite others into the life of Christ?

Many aspects of worship will need to be carefully planned and intentionally practiced. These include the call to worship, confessing the catholic creeds, congregational singing, giving offerings, passing the peace, pronouncing the benediction, and blessing the church as it is sent into the world.

Let's consider four means of grace Wesley most often noted: prayer, studying Scripture, participation in the Lord's Supper, and baptism. By expanding their significance, let's consider how they (and others) might serve the mission of evangelism.

WHICH CAME FIRST, THE CONVERSION OR THE PRACTICE?

Growing up in the Christian faith, I thought the way most people came to faith in Jesus was through an intellectual presentation that culminates in the confession of sin and a public affirmation of faith. That led me to learn methods that would convince someone to "believe in Jesus." After that, they would *then* learn the practices of faith. If that went well, they could contemplate church membership. Although that worked well in some instances, I am increasingly convinced that for most people, Christian conversion is a "messy and complicated" process. It is highly doubtful that a person will come to Christian faith apart from a friendship or relationship with a member of Christ's body. My experience is that most new Christians participated in the practices of faith before confessing personal faith in Christ. The practices were instrumental in their moving toward faith.

Here are two personal examples. Of the many labels I might embrace for myself—son, husband, father, pastor, and teacher—a handful resulted from a kind of "conversion." Two of these are scholar and exerciser (as in health-conscious person).

Becoming a scholar took a lot of time. It happened quite naturally and accidentally. Like most people, as a child I was taught to do things scholars do: read, write, and try to communicate my thoughts coherently and persuasively. But I did these things more because of coercion than because of love. I studied to pass a course and eventually earn a degree. I hoped this would lead to gainful employment. At some point (later than it should have been) a switch turned on; what I had been doing out of duty became habitual and desirable. I can't explain all of the reasons. Some of it had to do with being in relationship with scholars who modeled the joy of reading, writing, and giving thoughtful lectures. Some of it had to do with reading transformative or writing well-received research papers or the joy of teaching new insights to others. I can't explain it, and I don't know the date. But somewhere amid participating in the practices of a learning community, I quit just "going to school." I became a lifelong student and, in some measure, a scholar.

Similarly, I was "converted" to a healthier lifestyle through practices and relationships. There is one key difference, however. I did not know that I needed to become a scholar—that came as a surprise. I knew I needed to become healthier, but I didn't fully know how. So I went somewhere the healthy people in my life frequented: I visited a local gym. I have been a runner on and off throughout my life. But I had never really been a gym person. At first the practices were foreign to me; many of them still are. I tried a spin class because a friend invited me and because, observing through the window the people sweating on their stationary bikes to the beat of music, it actually looked like fun. On my first day I could not have felt more awkward. It took exactly thirty seconds for the instructor to know I was "in over my head." She gave me some initial instructions. She also gently encouraged me not to become discouraged and not to try everything the others were doing. "Do as much as you can without killing yourself," she said. It took me the first seven minutes of an hour-long class to reach the limit of my abilities as a beginner.

My spin experience was replicated in a couple of other exercise courses and on the gym's treadmills, moving staircases, and weight machines. In those first weeks I felt as conspicuous and awkward as a seventh grader on the first day in junior high. But thanks to some patient instructors, diligent trainers, and kind colaborers, I have begun to get the hang of gym life. I'm not sure I can claim full conversion status to athlete or even to being a healthy person. But I am on the road to redemption and belonging!

Being "converted" to scholarship and working out pales in comparison with "the surpassing value of knowing Christ Jesus my Lord" (Phil. 3:8, NRSV). However, the process is comparable. I did not begin to believe in the life of the scholar and athlete and then learn the related practices. The practices of academe and gym were part and parcel of my conversion process. The same is true for the majority of persons who come to faith.

After thirty years of ministry, I have yet to persuade someone to come to faith by using argumentation and subsequently introducing him or her to the church's practices and means of grace. Quite the opposite is true. Everyone I have aided in coming to faith in Christ has entered (at least in part) through the means of grace. For instance, think of prayer not only as a way to advance in faith but also as an important means by which someone might come to faith.

Prayer

In Matthew 6 and Luke 11 Jesus teaches his disciples how to pray. In the Lukan account the conversation begins with a question from the disciples. "He was praying in a certain place, and after he had finished, one his disciples said to him, 'Lord, teach us to pray, as John taught his disciples'" (11:1, NRSV). What seems significant is that not only did the disciples want to learn to pray, but they also wanted to pray in a way that would help people recognize them as Jesus's followers. As they learned to pray in this way, people would know that they were the Lord's disciples.

In Matthew and Luke, the Lord's Prayer contains at least six key elements:

- Hallowing or making sacred the Lord's name
- Inviting or imploring the coming of God's kingdom ("on earth as it is in heaven" [Matt. 6:10, NRSV])
- A request for daily provision
- Confession of sin
- Extending to others the grace we have received
- And an urgent call for the Lord to be present and deliver us from times of trial (and "from the evil one" [Matt. 6:13, NRSV])

Although there are forms of prayer not associated with a worship service, such as a prayer of confession and a prayer for illumination, let's focus on a prayer of intercession. In intercessory prayer, God's people assume the priestly function of offering the frequently broken, sinful, and hurting world to God. Then they extend the healing, blessing, and peacemaking presence of God to the world. Theology is richly embodied in intercessory prayer. It affirms that God knows and cares for all creation. It also embodies the hope that God can and often does act in ways that point toward God's final transformation of all things in the new creation. In prayer, many of our core faith convictions are embodied. James K. A. Smith says,

> Praying enacts an entire cosmology because implicit in the very act of prayer is an entire ontology[4] and construal of the God-world relationship. This doesn't mean that we need to pursue a doctorate in metaphysics in order to pray; on the contrary, the point is that by doing it, by praying, we are engaged in a sort of performative ontology that could be teased out in reflection and analysis.[5]

The phone rang late at night. It was our neighbor Tina, calling from the hospital. She and her husband had become Christians a few months earlier. They came to faith and had been baptized after their children were invited by our children to vacation Bible school. VBS led to the family attending on Sunday mornings. The combination of regular participation in worship and friendship with us eventually led to a confession of Christian faith.

Tina was calling because another couple in our subdivision, whom we did not know, had just given birth to a premature baby; the prognosis was grim. Tina knew the parents, Scott and Stephanie, through the local kid's baseball league. She heard through the grapevine that baby Savannah had arrived several weeks early. Tina rushed to the hospital and walked into the room just as the doctor was explaining how the proteins in Savannah's blood were beginning to attach to her tiny organs. Savannah's survival through the night was unlikely. The doctor encouraged them to make calls to family members and encourage them to come quickly. She also encouraged them to call their pastor if they had one. If not, the hospital chaplain could be requested. Through tears, Stephanie said their family was on the way. But she didn't have a pastor. Tina spoke up. "I have one!" That is why she was now in the hallway calling me.

"Would you come and pray for Savannah?" she asked.

"Of course," I replied. "I'll be right there."

Before she hung up, she added, "And could you bring some of that oil stuff with you?"

Debbie and I made our way to the hospital to pray for Savannah. I was trying to overcome the awkwardness of walking into a situation where I didn't know anyone. I was also battling my own fears and lack of faith as I wondered how best to pray for Savannah. What might I hope for God to do? One of my most vivid pastoral memories is holding that less-than-two-pound baby in the palm of my hand and praying that God would be gracious to Savannah. I asked God to sustain her life. I prayed, regardless of the outcome, that God would surround Scott and Stephanie with his presence and that they would know his comfort and strength. After prayer and conversation, Debbie and I left.

Early the next morning we received a call from the hospital. It was Stephanie telling me that Savannah had survived the night. She was beginning to show small signs of improvement. Stephanie didn't want to impose, but she wondered if I might come to the hospital again to pray for Savannah and her family (she also asked me to bring that "oil stuff"). I agreed and went to the hospital immediately. In coming days and weeks, I would be there frequently. I would repeatedly pray for Savannah as she grew stronger. In the meantime, prayer requests for Savannah made the all-church prayer list. Prayers for her became part of our intercessory prayers on Sunday mornings. Added to that were dozens of casseroles and meals prepared by loving Christians whom Scott and Stephanie had never met.

In time, Scott and Stephanie came to faith. They were baptized the following Easter. Savannah's presence in church was just a few weeks later on Mother's Day. Her arrival came with a standing ovation by the congregation. There were prayers of thanksgiving to God. Savannah is now a college student.

I will be eternally grateful for God's faithful guidance in those circumstances. I tell the story simply to point out that Scott and Stephanie did not come to faith and then learn how to pray. They began to pray, to make space in their lives for a God they did not yet fully know, and then they came to faith. They witnessed a community of people—a kingdom of priests—offering to God the pain of a little girl and the fears of her parents. Then they offered the presence of God's Holy Spirit to Stephanie and Scott. Congregational prayer was not offered in response to parental faith; it became the pathway to their faith.

The Study of Scripture, the Lord's Supper, and Baptism

Much can be said to commend private and corporate study of Scripture. It is, indeed, "useful for teaching, for reproof, for correction, and for training in righteousness" (2 Tim. 3:16, NRSV). But how does the Bible become the foundational story that forms how God's people see, understand, and interpret their lives in the world? The Word of God is not a source from which to extract a list of religious propositions believers must affirm. Rather, as James K. A. Smith notes, "The Scriptures function as the script of the worshiping community, the story that narrates the identity of the people of God, the constitution of this baptismal city, and the fuel of the Christian imagination."[6] In other words, the study of Scripture involves much more than "knowing." It is a means of grace that creates a new way of seeing. Perhaps that's why there are so many stories in the Bible about blind people being healed.

My favorite ethicist, Alasdair MacIntyre, is known for the following quote: "I can only answer the question, 'What am I to do?' if I can answer the prior question, 'Of what story or stories do I find myself a part?'"[7] His point is that we are all "storied" creatures. We can't keep from living into some kind of storied or narrative understanding of the world, our existence and place within it. All sorts of stories are at work in our world today. Some people live the "success story" or the "sensuality story." Others give themselves to a story of nationalism or humanism. Many people live a nihilistic story, for they believe life is thoroughly accidental. There are no moral norms or values applicable to all persons. There is no story by which to live. Ironically, "there is no story" becomes their "story."

By contrast, study of Scripture privately and corporately offers the world a counterstory, a story of God's creation, redemption, and renewal of all things. In the light of Scripture's profound, true, and beautiful story, all competing stories are forms of idolatry.

Debbie, my wife, came to Christian faith providentially and accidentally. She exited the freeway at the wrong place and just happened to pass by a church she thought looked beautiful and inviting. She decided to attend the next Sunday. She owned no Bible and knew very little about Christianity. In fact, when the pastor (my father) opened the altar for prayer at the end of the service, Debbie panicked. The only altars she knew about were found in movies where animals or virgins were sacrificed. Thankfully my dad felt checked. He explained the altar was a safe place. If we sensed God was drawing us, we could respond by moving toward him.

That morning, on hearing her first sermon, Debbie thought the text was telling the story of her life and her need. She knew almost nothing about the overall Christian story. But what she had heard resonated with her. She knew immediately that she must abandon the broken, untruthful story she had been living. She knew she must enter the truth-full and life-giving story of Jesus.

I have witnessed the effectiveness of the sacraments of baptism and the Lord's Supper not only in the continued transformation of Christians but also in evangelism.

Wesleyan theologian Brent Peterson maintains, "The Lord's Supper is a primary sacrament for people becoming more fully human, for the further healing of creation, and for the further coming of the kingdom of God."[8] Lisa had been attending our college ministry services for several months when after a service that ended at the Eucharistic Table, she came to me in tears. "I get it now!" she said. "I've never truly felt a part of my family. Tonight, I realized for the first time that I am now part of a new family—the family of God."

CONCLUSION

Each time I read Paul's statement in Romans 6, that all who have been baptized into Christ Jesus were baptized into his death "so that, just as Christ was raised from the dead by the glory of the Father, so we too might walk in newness of life" (v. 4, NRSV), I think of my friend Ryan. After years of professed agnosticism, Ryan came to faith in Christ. After his baptism he framed his baptismal document and surrounded it with candles. I asked why he had built this little shrine to his baptism. "This new creation life is hard," Ryan replied. "So, each morning I light these candles and remind myself that I am a new creation."

Stories of growth in grace by believers and of effective evangelism through the means of grace abound. I close by affirming again that the church will be formed and fulfill its mission by its practices of the faith. With Wesley, I reject empty formalism that "mistake[s] the *means* for the *end*."[9] However, also like Wesley, I fear that when the historic and biblical means of grace are neglected, not only is the growth of current followers of Jesus likely anemic, but also we are neglecting primary ways people can witness themselves "practiced" into faith and trust in Christ.

Questions for Consideration

1. Is inviting non-Christians to join a congregation in the "practice of the faith" an invitation to hypocrisy?
2. In what ways can services of worship in your congregation incorporate additional means of grace?
3. Does inviting others to participate in "practicing the faith" rule out explicitly telling others about the good news of Jesus Christ and inviting them to become Christians?

Additional Resources

Blevins, Dean. "On Wesleyan Discipleship: Seven-Minute Seminary." Published on August 30, 2016. Seedbed video, 7:41. https://www.youtube.com/watch?v=drvbrwdy6r8.

Bryant, Barry E. "John Wesley on 'Searching the Scriptures': Reading, Meditating, Hearing, Doing." Oxford Institute of Methodist Theological Studies. https://oimts.files.wordpress.com/2013/04/2007-2-bryant.pdf.

Morgenthaler, Sally. *Worship Evangelism: Inviting Unbelievers into the Presence of God*. Grand Rapids: Zondervan, 1999.

Peterson, Brent D. *Created to Worship: God's Invitation to Become Fully Human* (Kansas City: Beacon Hill Press of Kansas City, 2012).

Wheeler, David, and Vernon M. Whaley. *The Great Commission to Worship: Biblical Principles for Worship-Based Evangelism*. Nashville: B and H Academic, 2011.

11

PRACTICAL APPLICATIONS

HOLINESS TODAY INTERVIEW WITH MARK BANE AND SCOTT RAINEY

A well-built house always starts with a solid foundation. Jesus reminded his followers of this truth with the parable of the wise and foolish builders (Matt. 7:24-27). The wise man understood the importance of a solid foundation, so he built his house on solid rock. The rain and wind were no match for the stability of a rock foundation. The foolish man, on the other hand, used sand for his foundation. The rain and the wind quickly demolished his poorly constructed house.

This book has laid a solid theological foundation to guide our ministries as we fulfill the Great Commission of Jesus: "Therefore go and make disciples of all nations, baptizing them in the name of the Father and of the Son and of the Holy Spirit, and teaching them to obey everything I have commanded you. And surely I am with you always, to the very end of the age" (28:19-20, NIV). This command challenges us to build on a solid foundation with action steps. This book explores the hands and feet of evangelism. It challenges us to find ways to apply the theological principles of evangelism to our daily lives and to witness for Jesus Christ.

Holiness Today (HT) invited two directors from the Global Ministry Center of the Church of the Nazarene to answer a series of questions that lead to tangible applications for the information found in this book. These applications work with a variety of ministries in the local church and in the lives of Christ's followers. Mark Bane (MB) serves as director of Evangelism and New Church Development for the Church of the Nazarene USA/Canada. Scott Rainey (SR) serves as global director for Sunday School and Discipleship Ministries International for the Church of the Nazarene. Both men have a wealth of experience in applying theological insights of evangelism and discipleship to daily living. They both also carry a heavy burden for lost people and desire to see as many men, women, youth, and children as possible in a loving relationship with Jesus Christ.

Before turning to the interview questions, we need to define a couple of terms used by the directors: "evangelism" and "discipleship." "Evangelism" is the relational, spiritual direction for a person who is ready to repent and trust Jesus for salvation. This readiness to help comes from a Spirit-led sensitivity to the unsaved along their journey of faith. "Discipleship" is the systematic journey with an individual from no faith to new faith to deepening faith.

HT: What are some of your life applications that connect biblical and theological principles of evangelism to local church ministry?

MB: I believe every local church must intentionally foster a vision for organizational seriousness about evangelism. By this I mean that every pastor, church member, formation group, and ministry of a local congregation must be laser focused with a passion to reach lost people. We must move beyond conversations, intentions, and dreams to practical methods of intersecting the lives of people who need to know Jesus as their personal Savior.

This level of determination and intentionality must find tangible expressions in the daily schedules of Christ's followers. All believers must commit to intentional efforts to engage in conversations with lost people regularly. This includes circling back to reconnect with lost friends from previous interactions last week or last month. We must have proper motives in interacting regularly with lost people. We should never trivialize them by perceiving them as nothing more than a potential customer of our religious faith, another person to count in our statistics, or another potential financial contributor to our church. In other words, we do not engage with people simply to "close the deal" or to get them to make a simple instantaneous commitment that they regret the next morning. That sort of mindset misses the entire purpose of evangelism. It misuses people by valuing them only for our intention to count them as witnessing results. However, the above statement must be balanced with the biblical facts. What is the nature of this balance?

On the one hand, we know we are to love others as Jesus loved them. He lived among people, healed them of their diseases, fed them when hungry, and served them in many ways. Jesus, John, and Paul consistently lived their witness in the world and admonished us to follow their examples.

1. Jesus told us to love others as ourselves (Matthew 22:37-39).
2. John told us to love in actions and truth rather than just word and speech (1 John 3:18).
3. Paul lived, debated, and used convincing arguments with many people through his missionary journeys recorded in the book of Acts.

On the other hand, Scripture reminds us of the importance of making disciples.

1. Jesus said, "Therefore go make disciples" (Matt. 28:19, NIV).
2. Jesus said, "Go out to the roads and country lanes and compel them to come in" (Luke 14:23, NIV).
3. Paul said, "Since, then, we know what it is to fear the Lord, we try to persuade others" (2 Cor. 5:11, NIV).
4. Peter said, "[The Lord] is patient with you, not wanting anyone to perish, but everyone to come to repentance" (2 Pet. 3:9, NIV; see also Matt. 18:14).
5. Jesus met the woman in Samaria, loved her, told her the truth about her life, and brought her into the kingdom in one visit at the well (John 4:1-42).
6. Jesus met Matthew the tax collector and called him to follow him in their very first meeting (Matt. 9:9-13).

7. Philip led the Ethiopian eunuch to faith in a onetime encounter (Acts 8:26-40).

We must value people as image-bearing creatures of God and treat them with dignity and respect as we are present in their lives and as we proclaim the good news to them. We should also recognize that our mission is to partner with the Spirit in the mission to ensure that none perish (2 Pet. 3:9). We must always remember that people with whom we engage have eternal souls. They carry a level of guilt and perhaps shame over life's sins and failures. We believe everyone needs Jesus. He wants to forgive their sins and transform their lives by the indescribable power of the gospel. God offers us an opportunity to join with him in finding lost people who need to know him as personal Lord and Savior. This motivates our evangelism efforts.

The enemy will do everything possible to keep us from fostering a personal interest in lost people. He has no problem with our community connections and our involvement in all manner of service projects. This is not intended to be an indictment against service to the needy or compassionate ministries. Nevertheless, these worthy efforts must never replace the central importance of our personal Christian testimony. Our witness to the transforming power of the gospel of Jesus Christ threatens the enemy. Thus he fights vigorously against our evangelistic efforts.

SR: Conversations between Christian believers exhibit a renewed interest in the spiritual gifts listed in passages such as Romans 12, 1 Corinthians 12, and Ephesians 4. The gift of evangelism appears on these lists, with some Christians possessing that spiritual gift, while others do not. Researchers conclude that about 10 percent of believers have the gift of evangelism. Even if 90 percent of Christians today do not believe they have the spiritual gift of evangelism, that does not mean they are exempt from the responsibility of being involved personally in God's mission to the world. In the Great Commission, Jesus clearly invites everyone to participate in his divine initiative. Acts 1:8 is a reminder that "you will receive power when the Holy Spirit comes on you; and you will be my witnesses in Jerusalem, and in all Judea and Samaria, and to the ends of the earth" (NIV). The entire book of Jonah provides a clear picture of God's interest in having a relationship with everyone in the world. God deeply desired for the Ninevites to repent and believe in him and worked through Jonah's reluctance to declare the word of the Lord to the citizens of Nineveh.

The busyness of life often crowds our schedules with too many things to accomplish in a given day. It is easy for Christians to use the excuse of an overcrowded schedule to pass the responsibility of discipleship and evangelism to someone else. As with Jonah's arguments, God does not find these excuses legitimate. God wants all of Christ's followers involved in his mission.

Lacking particular skills is not an excuse to avoid God's mission to our world. Scripture lists financial giving as a spiritual gift. The Lord blesses some people with an extraordinary capacity to generate money, and these individuals find ways to invest significant portions of this money in the kingdom work of the Lord. We are thankful for individuals with this gift who see their involvement in God's mission as part of their Christian service.

This does not mean, however, that only those with the special gift of giving contribute financially to the Lord's work. God challenges all of us to contribute financially to kingdom work according to our ability (2 Cor. 8:10-12). In that same way, God challenges all of us to find ways to participate in discipleship and evangelism ministries. First Peter 4:10 reminds us, "Each of you should use whatever gift you have received to serve others, as faithful stewards of God's grace in its various forms" (NIV).

HT: What does a practical application of the theological foundations in this book look like in the life of a local church?

SR: Pastor and congregation must build a level of trust and confidence in one another to function together as a team. Good team dynamics within this group will find ways to apply the principles of this book to the life of any local church. Team members must think and plan together for each member to use his or her gifts, regardless of what those gifts from God might be, for discipleship and evangelistic ministries.

Many churches invest a great deal of time and effort into providing a strong Sunday school ministry. Leaders within these churches locate high-quality teachers for various age groups, train them, and then empower them to lead weekly Sunday school class sessions. This system provides accountability for class members and creates a natural system for involving class leaders in the lives, circumstances, and difficulties that class members experience in daily life. Weekly Bible study and participation together within a small group community of faith provides an excellent nurturing environment for believers to grow in their faith.

While most Sunday school classes today primarily serve Christians with opportunities to grow in their faith and their accountability to others within the group, teachers and class members must remember that a call to make disciples (the heart of Sunday school) should always include the desire to reach lost people. Sunday school teachers must understand that their role is not to just make disciples but to make disciple makers of the members of their classes. Of course, each local congregation must go beyond Sunday school efforts and ensure that every ministry of the local church is engaged in outreach to lost people. In our contemporary society, it seems that very few lost people will make their way to churches in order for believers to present them with the gospel message. Therefore, if they do not come to us, we have a responsibility as the body of Christ to go out into the world and find them.

MB: Every local church, regardless of its age, regional location, or social setting, has an intricate web of systems, habits, and behaviors that uniquely identify it. All of these factors work together to create a ministry profile within a local community. That profile, in large part, sets the stage for the level of engagement with the community for effective evangelism ministries. Some churches exist to maintain the status quo with the systems, habits, and behaviors that have characterized them for years, even decades. Churches with this operational mode seldom effectively evangelize their local communities.

Local church leaders must make a conscious effort to examine every system, habit, and behavior to assure that each one contributes to the mission of bringing lost people to Christ and discipling them in their faith. We must replace activities and practices that do not pass this examination with those that highly value lost people and nurture their spiritual development.

Many local churches do commendable work in offering ministries and worship services that attract new people. The attractional model of ministry often accomplishes its purpose in drawing new people to visit local churches. It fails to accomplish its intended purpose, however, if Christ's followers do not somehow take additional steps to make personal connections with these visitors. It also fails because most people in our communities will not visit a church, but they might engage with faith as a result of a friendship established completely outside the context of a church service. We must not choose between inviting them to church or going out and meeting them where they are. We must do both. Therefore, we must not choose between providing an attractional ministry or living faith out in daily interactions with them in their own environments. We must do both.

If and when visitors come, we must introduce ourselves to them and get to know them personally by name. Beyond that, we must learn family members' names as we take an interest in the many facets of their lives. We must take them to dinner and learn their history. Through time and personal investment of ourselves with them, we develop relationships that naturally lead to sharing the good news of Jesus Christ with them.

HT: How do the theological principles presented in this book manifest themselves in the pastor's ministry?

MB: The pastor must find ways to weave the principles of this book into sermons. For example, a pastor might promote an evangelistic emphasis by preaching a series of sermons from the book of Acts. This book illustrates the work of the Holy Spirit in evangelism through a wide variety of people in many different settings. The real-life examples in the book of Acts put flesh and bone on nearly every principle of discipleship and evangelism.

The pastor can also seek ways to weave the principles of this book into daily conversations with laypeople. We often characterize people according to the topics of conversation they most often discuss. Some people enjoy discussing work projects, leisure activities, or vacation outings with family members. Without being overbearing or obnoxious about it, ministers have opportunities to promote discussions with lay leaders about the needs of lost people within communities. This may lead naturally to discussions of effective ways of reaching out to them with the good news of the gospel.

Furthermore, the pastor must model evangelism (personal disciple making) in his or her own life. In other words, the pastor must make a priority of finding pre-Christians, engaging them in conversation, and leading them to faith. The duties and responsibilities of a pastor require daily attention; much of a pastor's work exemplifies a good use of time and effort. At the end of the day, however, no amount of busy activity replaces the absolute necessity of intersecting lost people's lives with the hope found in Jesus.

Along with personally leading people to Christ, the pastor can place special emphasis on personal transformation stories by interviewing new believers in a morning worship service. The excitement generated through testimonies of new believers, presented in their own words, can breathe new life into the corporate worship of any congregation. These interviews also assist the pastor in influencing the conversation of the local church. When the pastor talks about changed lives on a regular basis, church members hear this priority reinforced and see it as possible.

SR: I agree with everything Mark has said. I would like to add one additional thought. The pastor is always the primary leader in making sure that discipleship and evangelism receive the central focus they deserve within the congregation. The pastor must mastermind the plan of discipleship and evangelism that will be implemented within the congregation. The pastor must always lead and promote these priorities in order for them to be infused into the personality of the local church.

HT: How do the theological principles presented in this book manifest themselves in local church boards and leaders?

SR: Church boards usually assign members to subcommittees that represent responsibilities for the operation of a local church. Common subcommittees include finance, Christian education, building and grounds, missions, and so on. The pastor and lay leaders must incorporate a laser-focused emphasis on discipleship and evangelism within each subcommittee. Placing someone with both a gifting and a passion for discipleship and evangelism on each subcommittee helps promote the emphasis through local church ministries.

The "discipleship and evangelism" advocate on the finance committee might frequently ask the group how local church expenditures reflect the congregation's outreach priorities. The advocate on the Christian education committee might ask what role members ought to assume in providing high-quality training for more effective outreach. The advocate on the building and grounds committee might ask how facilities within the buildings or the buildings themselves that are located in the community might better minister to the lost people of the area. The advocate on the missions committee might consider the mission of the denomination, "to make Christlike disciples in the nations,"[1] and reflect on how members might apply this vision on the local level. Every leader in the local church must constantly give attention to the question, "How can we better reach the lost in this community?"

MB: A movement of God in a local congregation that draws believers into the mission of God starts small. By this I mean that God's vision usually starts in the heart of the pastor. From there, God reaches through the pastor to the influential leaders of the congregation. Once leaders catch the vision, it often quickly spreads through the personal connections of these leaders to an entire host of believers in the congregation. This vision then leads the entire congregation out into their spheres of personal influence with the people they encounter on a daily basis in their neighborhoods, schools, and jobs.

Church board meeting agendas reflect pastoral and lay-leader priorities. Financial statistics, attendance trends, and building maintenance represent three subjects that nearly always find high priority on church board agendas. An additional item needs to appear at the beginning of every church board meeting agenda: disciple making. God did not call us to only make agendas, plan worship services, have great facilities, provide great music, and preach practical sermons. All of these activities will exist in a healthy Church of the Nazarene. However, they are not the mission of the church. God commissioned us to make Christlike disciples. Often this mission gets lost in the minutiae of daily ministry, planning, and activity. Board members must discuss this topic on a monthly basis with a series of questions:

1. What efforts did we make this month at disciple making?
2. If our disciple-making efforts have no tangible evidence, why not?
3. How can we best correct this situation in order to see new people brought to Christ and nurtured in their faith?

A local church pastor should never attempt to cast this evangelistic vision to the entire congregation before laying the essential groundwork with lay leaders. This groundwork brings key leaders within the congregation up to speed on the vision God has given the pastor. Regular discussions and extended seasons of prayer together help solidify God's evangelistic vision with the pastor and the people.

HT: Some argue that evangelism is culturally inappropriate for the twenty-first century. How do you answer that assessment?

SR: Christian believers for many years have tended to think of evangelism coming first in reaching lost people. Once individuals decide to follow Christ, we then introduce them to discipleship ministries that help them grow and mature in the Christian faith. Aspects of contemporary society that exhibit an anti-Christian perspective reject the entire notion of Christian evangelism. They perceive it as nothing more than trying to get people to join a particular social group or a religious organization.

Perhaps the time has arrived for us to break out of this paradigm and adopt a new one. We might want to begin thinking of evangelism happening best somewhere on the continuum of discipleship. By that I mean that we begin our discipleship ministry to lost people before they accept Jesus as Lord and Savior. We are not the first generation to think in this way. Christians adopted this paradigm hundreds of years prior to us.

Let me illustrate what I mean with an example from the home environment. Christian parents "disciple" their children from birth to adulthood. This discipleship regimen occurs naturally in family life. Parents pray with their children before meals and at bedtime. They read Bible stories to them throughout the day. They talk to them about the fingerprint of God in the beauty they see in nature as they walk together through the park. They teach their children to trust their lives to the Lord during difficult circumstances in life. The everyday routines in the home can become teaching moments for parents.

Without a doubt, the Holy Spirit uses all of these parental ministries to speak softly into the hearts of children. Parents introduce all the components of God's salvation story at the appropriate time in children's lives. It is a natural conversation between parent and child. Somewhere on this journey, parents talk to their children about the need to repent of their sins and ask Jesus into their hearts. No parent ever says, "I do not have the gift of evangelism, so I cannot talk to my child about Jesus." Evangelism in the home is not an external activity imposed upon a Christian parent. It flows naturally in the everyday give-and-take of life.

Now apply that illustration from family life to the way Christians think about lost people within their communities and spheres of influence. We can look for opportunities to season our everyday conversations with the life-transforming claims of the gospel message. We can offer to pray for the special needs of friends who do not know Jesus as their personal Savior. We can seize the moment and pray for them on the spot by asking, "May I offer a word of prayer right now for your special need?" Most people welcome the opportunity to have someone take a personal interest in their situation. As our friends hear the words we pray, they hear the language of our faith that speaks of a personal relationship with the Lord.

We can also talk to people about what the Bible says about God's willingness to be involved in meeting our needs. We can call attention to answers to those prayers and remind our friends of God's intervention in their life circumstances. All of these activities represent preconversion discipleship opportunities that open people's hearts and minds to the idea of God's love for them.

As we build meaningful relationships with lost people, we can listen for the promptings of the Holy Spirit. We count on the fact that his work in the lives of these individuals has gone before us. He has been preparing their hearts for the message of good news. We listen for the promptings of the Spirit to indicate when we are to speak evangelistically. Our words flow naturally in the relationships we have developed. They speak to the deepest needs of other hearts hungry for the hope that only Christ brings. Just as with the illustration about parents and children, our presentation of the gospel occurs in a very natural way on the discipleship continuum.

We must find natural and winsome ways to connect with lost people. For many years we promoted something known as "cold-turkey calling." That is, we went two by two to the doors of total strangers and presented the gospel message. Perhaps that method proved effective in bygone days, but no more. Today, we must develop meaningful relationships with people, earn the right to speak with them on a personal level, and then share the gospel from a heart filled with love and concern for them.

We are not offering a new concept to Wesleyan Christians. Wesleyan's have always understood this perspective as one of the many manifestations of God's prevenient grace. God uses believers to intersect the lives of lost people with whom he has been involved for a long time. Sometimes we speak of discipleship and evangelism by saying, "The church has a mission." Actually, a better way to express this thought is to say, "God's mission has a church." He invites us to participate in this mission to the world.

MB: A quick review of church history tells us that cultures around the world in every century have considered evangelism and disciple making inappropriate. The arguments used today against bringing pre-Christians to faith are as old as God's mission in our world. Detractors have always found the Christian priority of engaging lost people with the good news of the gospel offensive. Authentic Christianity is rarely popular; popular Christianity is rarely authentic.

I do not know this as a certain fact, but I suspect that cultural rejections of discipleship and evangelism flow from the exclusive nature of the Christian message. Jesus said, "I am the way and the truth and the life. No one comes to the Father except through me" (John 14:6, NIV). Such a bold, exclusive statement offends many postmodern ears. Ours is an age of inclusion, of tolerance for all beliefs and positions, and of valuing all belief systems as equally valid. The Christian message centers on our Lord and Savior Jesus Christ. It costs believers everything when they surrender their lives at the foot of the cross. Peter reinforced this understanding when he said, "Salvation is found in no one else, for there is no other name under heaven given to mankind by which we must be saved" (Acts 4:12, NIV). Paul reminds us that "at the name of Jesus every knee should bow, in heaven and on earth and under the earth, and every tongue acknowledge that Jesus Christ is Lord, to the glory of God the Father" (Phil. 2:10-11, NIV).

May God empower us to join effectively in his mission to the world as we apply the theological principles of this book to our daily lives and the corporate life of our local churches.

NOTES

Introduction

1. Emil Bruner, *The Word and the World* (London: Student Christian Movement Press, 1931), 108.

2. The five discourses are as follows: (1) the Sermon on the Mount (Matt. 5:1–7:27); (2) missionary instructions (chap. 10); (3) collection of parables (chap. 13); (4) sayings on humility and forgiveness (community instructions) (chap. 18); and (5) sermon on eschatology (chaps. 23–25).

3. Bryan P. Stone, *Evangelism after Christendom: The Theology and Practice of Christian Witness* (Grand Rapids: Brazos Press, 2007), 12.

4. Alan Kreider, *The Patient Ferment of the Early Church: The Improbable Rise of Christianity in the Roman Empire* (Grand Rapids: Baker Academic, 2016), 129, 155.

5. Strategies and methods for evangelism are important. They just aren't this book's purpose.

Chapter 1

1. For her actions, in 1570 Pope Pius V declared Elizabeth a heretic. He judged her to be the "servant of crime."

2. The 1662 Act mandated the form of prayers, administration of the sacraments, and other rites of the established church. Dissenting came at the price of being excluded from public office.

3. "Articles of Religion," Historical Documents of the Church, in *The (Online) Book of Common Prayer* (New York: Church Hymnal Corporation, 2007), 867-76, https://www.bcponline.org/.

4. *Lex orandi, lex credendi* isn't limited to Anglicans. "The law of prayer is the law of faith" is also affirmed by Roman Catholics. The *Catechism of the Catholic Church* says that when celebrating the Eucharist, the church, in faith, is engaged in believing as she prays. The church "believes as she prays." The sacraments "presuppose faith" in the Word of God. *Catechism of the Catholic Church*, pt. 2, sec. 1, art. 2, subs. III, paras. 1122-24, http://www.vatican.va/archive/ENG0015/__P32.HTM.

5. The Homilies exhort to sound doctrine and exemplary Christian conduct.

6. The description doesn't do justice to the current unrest among Anglicans and the precipitous decline of church attendance in Great Britain. Peter Hitchens, columnist for *The Mail on Sunday*, paints a picture of religious "indifference" in Great Britain among Catholics and Anglicans. "Nobody cares about the great issues of the Reformation because nobody cares about God." Peter Hitchens, "Latimer and Ridley Are Forgotten," *First Things*, June/July 2018, 33-40, 39.

7. Interestingly, Anglicans and Methodists in Great Britain are on the verge of reuniting. On February 12, 2018, a Church of England general synod overwhelmingly backed plans to reunite the two churches.

8. Article 17: "Predestination to Life is the everlasting purpose of God, whereby (before the foundations of the world were laid) he hath constantly decreed by his counsel secret to us, to deliver from curse and damnation those whom he hath chosen in Christ out of mankind, and to bring them by Christ to everlasting salvation, as vessels made to honour. Wherefore, they which are endued with so excellent a benefit of God, be called according to God's purpose by his Spirit working in due season; they through Grace obey the calling; they be justified freely; they be made sons of God by adoption; they be made like the image of his only-begotten Son Jesus Christ; they walk religiously in good works, and at length, by God's mercy, they attain to everlasting felicity." *(Online) Book of Common Prayer*, 871.

9. John Wesley was strongly influenced by the Dutch theologian Jacobus Arminius (1560–1609). Wesleyans are known as "Arminians." But the designation is not to be confused with a form of liberal Arminianism that aligned with the teaching of Pelagius (ca. AD 360–ca. AD 418). The latter denied original sin and taught that in their own strength persons are free to obey the law and turn to Christ in faith. The will is free to exercise faith without divine assistance. Wesleyans reject Pelagianism in all forms, accept the reality of original sin that enslaves the will

toward God, and teach that only by the Holy Spirit's preparation and enablement can a penitent sinner receive and exercise the gift of faith. Salvation is by grace through faith alone, not by human effort in any form. Unfortunately, many Wesleyans carelessly speak as Pelagians and so misrepresent John and Charles Wesley, who were anchored in the Protestant Reformation.

10. *Catechism of the Catholic Church*, pt. 1, sec. 2, chap. 2, article 4, para. 2, subs. II, para. 605.

11. Charles Wesley, "Come, Sinners, to the Gospel Feast," in *Wesley Hymns*, comp. Ken Bible (Kansas City: Lillenas, 1982), no. 2.

12. John Wesley, "Free Grace," Sermon 128, in *The Sermons of John Wesley*, ed. Thomas Jackson (1872; Wesley Center Online, 1999), http://wesley.nnu.edu/john-wesley/the-sermons-of-john-wesley-1872-edition/sermon-128-free-grace/.

13. Here is an instance where Wesleyan theology is more compatible with Roman Catholic theology than it is with those Protestants who teach that salvation is limited only to the elect. The *Catechism of the Catholic Church* states, "The *preparation of man* for the reception of grace is already a work of grace. This latter is needed to arouse and sustain our collaboration in justification through faith, and in sanctification through charity." *Catechism of the Catholic Church*, pt. 3, sec. 1, chap. 3, art. 2, subs. II, para. 2001.

Although there were Methodists such as George Whitefield (1714-70) and Selina Hastings (1707-91), Countess of Huntingdon, who taught predestination (salvation provided only for the elect), Methodism followed John and Charles.

14. In 1784 John Wesley abridged the Anglican Articles of Religion for the Methodist Episcopal Church in America. He reduced to twenty-five the thirty-nine Anglican Articles of Religion. In addition to eliminating Articles that applied to the British context, Wesley eliminated the Calvinist interpretation of predestination.

15. John Wesley's 1784 abridgment of the Thirty-Nine Articles repeated Article 6 of the Thirty-Nine Articles as his Article 5.

16. Joel B. Green, "A Wesleyan Understanding of Biblical Authority: The Formation of Holy Lives," in *Square Peg: Why Wesleyans Aren't Fundamentalists* (Kansas City: Beacon Hill Press of Kansas City, 2012), 129. "What is needed most," Green says, "are people deeply embedded in faithful communities of discipleship, people in whom the Spirit is actualizing the Word of God and, thus, for whom the Word of God is authenticated. On the other hand, God speaks, and this is the basis for Scripture's authority. Through Scripture, God convinces us that

things between himself and humanity—indeed, between God and all creation—are just as we find in Scripture. Embracing Scripture's authority, we are drawn into the story of Scripture and especially more deeply into relationship with Scripture's primary character, God himself" (136).

17. John Wesley, preface to *Sermons on Several Occasions* (1771; repr., Christian Classics Ethereal Library [CCEL], n.d.), para. 5, https://ccel.org/ccel/wesley/sermons/sermons.iv.html.

18. John Wesley, ed., *A Christian Library*, 30 vols., 1821 ed., originally published in 50 vols. in 1750, Wesley Center Online, http://wesley.nnu.edu/john-wesley/a-christian-library-by-john-wesley/.

19. J. Ernest Rattenbury, *The Eucharistic Hymns of John and Charles Wesley* (London: Epworth Press, 1948), no. 42.

20. The text is poetic narrative.

21. Michael J. Gorman, *Inhabiting the Cruciform God: Kenosis, Justification, and Theosis in Paul's Narrative Soteriology* (Grand Rapids: Eerdmans, 2009), 9. Gorman identifies five echoes of scriptural images, as well as allusions to at least three cultural realities, that inform the text: (1) "preexistent Wisdom," (2) "the form and/or glory of God," (3) "Adam," (4) "the Isaianic suffering servant," and (5) "Israel's 'eschatological monotheism' within the framework of Isaiah 40–55 more generally" (14-15).

22. N. T. Wright, *The Climax of the Covenant* (Minneapolis: Fortress Press, 1993), 84, as quoted by Gorman, *Inhabiting the Cruciform God*, 9.

23. Wesley, "Salvation by Faith," Sermon 1, sec. 1, para. 5, in *The Sermons of John Wesley*, http://wesley.nnu.edu/john-wesley/the-sermons-of-john-wesley-1872-edition/sermon-1-salvation-by-faith/.

24. Wesley, "Catholic Spirit," Sermon 39, sec. 1, para. 11, in *The Sermons of John Wesley*, http://wesley.nnu.edu/john-wesley/the-sermons-of-john-wesley-1872-edition/sermon-39-catholic-spirit/.

25. David F. Watson, "Was Wesley's Faith a Creedal Faith?" *David F. Watson: Musings and Whatnot* (blog), April 8, 2015, https://davidfwatson.me/2015/04/08/was-wesleys-faith-a-creedal-faith/.

26. Wesley, "Catholic Spirit," sec. 3, para. 1.

27. John Wesley, *Explanatory Notes upon the New Testament* (1755; repr., Kansas City: Beacon Hill Press of Kansas City, 1981), comment on Rom. 12:6.

28. For example, for Anglicans, after the candidate for Christian baptism has been baptized, the congregation renews its baptismal vows in a baptismal

covenant, which consists of the Apostles' Creed. "The Baptismal Covenant," Holy Baptism, in *The (Online) Book of Common Prayer*, 304-5.

The twelve articles of the Apostles' Creed form the structure for pt. 1, sec. 2 of the *Catechism of the Catholic Church*, http://www.vatican.va/archive/ENG0015/_INDEX.HTM.

29. Some scholars say there are only three Articles in the Apostles' Creed: God the Father, Jesus Christ, and the Holy Spirit. That is how Ben Myers organizes *The Apostles' Creed: A Guide to the Ancient Catechism* (Bellingham, WA: Lexham Press, 2018). Relying on an early third-century document known as the *Apostolic Tradition*, Meyers describes candidates for baptism being charged to make three affirmations before being plunged three times into the baptismal waters. Each affirmation was similar to what Meyers sees as the three parts of the Apostles' Creed. Meyers, introduction to *Apostles' Creed*, https://www.amazon.com/Apostles-Creed-Catechism-Christian-Essentials/dp/1683590880/ref=sr_1_1?s=books&ie=UTF8&qid=1529674298&sr=1-1&keywords=Ben+Myers+The+Apostles+Creed&dpID=51r5U3J1XTL&preST=_SY291_BO1,204,203,200_QL40_&dpSrc=srch.

30. *The (Online) Book of Common Prayer*, 96.

31. A celebrated city of Asia, situated on the eastern side of Lake Ascania (currently Lake Iznik, Turkey) in Bithynia, built ca. 300 BC.

32. *The (Online) Book of Common Prayer*, 358-59.

33. The Council of Constantinople was convened to deal with the Macedonians or Pneumatomachians, who denied the deity of the Holy Spirit.

34. *The (Online) Book Common Pray*, 359.

35. Philip Schaff says, "There is no authentic evidence of an ecumenical recognition of this enlarged Creed till the Council at Chalcedon, 451, where it was read by Aëtius (a deacon of Constantinople) as the 'Creed of the 150 fathers,' and accepted as orthodox, together with the old Nicene Creed, or the 'Creed of the 318 fathers.'" *Creeds of Christendom, with a History and Critical Notes*, vol. 1, *The History of Creeds*, chap. 2, p. 46, CCEL, https://www.ccel.org/ccel/s/schaff/creeds1/cache/creeds1.pdf.

36. Philip Schaff, "Methodist Articles of Religion. A.D. 1784," in *The Creeds of the Evangelical Protestant Churches*, Part Third, https://biblehub.com/library/schaff/the_creeds_of_the_evangelical_protestant_churches/index.html. Wesley repeated the first of the Thirty-Nine Articles word for word.

37. Nestorius (ca. AD 386–450) and Eutyches (ca. AD 380–ca. AD 456) were the two Christian thinkers at the center of controversy that occasioned

Chalcedon. (1) Nestorius was a presbyter and monk in Antioch. In 428 he became patriarch of Constantinople. Although scholars debate what Nestorius actually taught, he so strongly emphasized the distinction between the divine and human natures in Christ that he left no room for the two natures to reside in one person, as the New Testament affirms. Consequently, Nestorius could not accept the communication of the two natures in one person (*communicatio idiomatum*). (2) Eutyches was an esteemed monastic superior in Constantinople. He insisted that Christ had only one nature. He taught the exclusive presence of the divine nature in Christ to the exclusion of the human. His teaching is known as *monophysitism* (*mono* [one] *physis* [nature]).

38. "Creed of Chalcedon," Early Church Creeds, Protestant Reformed Churches in America, http://www.prca.org/about/official-standards/creeds/ecumenical/chalcedon.

39. Schaff, "The Creed of Chalcedon," in vol. 1 of *Creeds of Christendom*, chap. 2, p. 54.

40. Ibid., 52. The "ancient church" applies to the Orthodox East and the Latin West. It overlooks the once-vast Nestorian and Jacobite Churches that thrived into the thirteenth century in regions such as Syria, Persia, Mesopotamia, India, Tibet, and China. That part of Christianity, now largely forgotten by Western Christians, accepted Nicaea but rejected the Chalcedonian affirmation of two natures in one person. They instead affirmed "one nature" in Christ and are by those who embrace Chalcedon referred to as "monophysites" (one nature). For an excellent treatment of this mostly forgotten and largely extinct part of historic Christianity, see Philip Jenkins, *The Lost History of Christianity* (New York: HarperOne, 2008). Jenkins observes, "Nestorians and Jacobites remained very influential for over eight hundred years after the great church councils expelled them . . . and they attracted believers over a huge geographical area" (27-28).

41. Henry H. Knight III and Douglas Powe Jr., *Transforming Evangelism: The Wesleyan Way of Sharing Faith* (Nashville: Discipleship Resources, 2006), 12.

42. Andy Johnson, *Holiness and the Missio Dei* (Eugene, OR: Cascade Books, 2016), 6.

43. Seven of the "I am" sayings have predicates: John 6:35; 8:12; 10:9, 11; 11:25-26; 14:6; 15:1. Other "I am" sayings are without predicates: 4:26; 6:20; 8:24, 28, 58; 13:19; 18:5.

44. Martin Luther said that if a person has been given "righteousness, life, and salvation by faith," he "cannot be restrained. He betrays himself. He breaks

out. He confesses and teaches this gospel to the people at the risk of life itself." Martin Luther, "Preface to the New Testament," in *Martin Luther: Selections from His Writings*, ed. John Dillenberger (Garden City, NY: Anchor Books, 1961), 17-18.

45. Phil Meadows, "Missional Discipleship in the Wesleyan Spirit," Catalyst: Contemporary Evangelical Perspective for Methodist Seminarians, posted March 30, 2016, http://www.catalystresources.org/missional-discipleship-in-the-wesleyan-spirit/.

46. Joseph Ratzinger, *Jesus of Nazareth, Part Two: Holy Week: From the Entrance into Jerusalem to the Resurrection* (San Francisco: Ignatius Press, 2011), 78.

47. Meadows, "Missional Discipleship in the Wesleyan Spirit." See John Wesley, "On Working Out Our Own Salvation," Sermon 85, in *The Sermons of John Wesley*, http://wesley.nnu.edu/john-wesley/the-sermons-of-john-wesley-1872-edition/sermon-85-on-working-out-our-own-salvation/.

48. Meadows, "Missional Discipleship in the Wesleyan Spirit." See John Wesley, "On Visiting the Sick," Sermon 98, in *The Sermons of John Wesley*, http://wesley.nnu.edu/john-wesley/the-sermons-of-john-wesley-1872-edition/sermon-98-on-visiting-the-sick/.

49. N. T. Wright, *The Day the Revolution Began: Reconsidering the Meaning of Jesus's Crucifixion* (New York: HarperOne, 2016), 365.

50. In the first five books (the Pentateuch) of the Greek Old Testament (the Septuagint), the expression "make perfect" (*teleioun*) means to "consecrate as priest." Ratzinger, *Jesus of Nazareth, Part Two: Holy Week*, 164.

Chapter 2

1. Frances Romero, "Top 10 U.N. General-Assembly Moments: Khrushchev Loses His Cool," *Time*, accessed November 1, 2018, http://content.time.com/time/specials/packages/article/0,28804,1843506_1843505_1843496,00.html.

2. Theodore Beza, quoted at Oxford Reference.com, accessed October 30, 2018, http://www.oxfordreference.com/view/10.1093/acref/9780199539536.001.0001/acref-9780199539536-e-365.

3. A helpful introduction to postmodernism is Joseph Natoli, *A Primer to Postmodernity* (Malden, MA: Blackwell, 1997).

4. The postmodern disposition also affects perceptions of moral norms. Sociologist Christian Smith and his colleagues report that "six out of ten of the emerging adults [18 to 24 years old] we interviewed . . . said morality is a personal

choice, entirely a matter of individual decision. Moral rights and wrongs are essentially matters of individual opinion, in their view. Furthermore, the general approach associated with this outlook is not to judge anyone else on moral matters, since they are entitled to their own personal opinions, and not to let oneself be judged by anyone else." Christian Smith, Kari Christoffersen, Hilary Davidson, and Patricia Herzog, *Lost in Transition: The Dark Side of Emerging Adulthood* (Oxford, UK: Oxford University Press, 2011), 21.

5. Sociologists define "social location" as one's position in a social system that reflects a worldview, a perception of how things work, what is real, where things belong, and how they fit together. Everyone is "socially located" in some way.

6. "Attendance at Religious Services," Religion and Public Life, Pew Research Center, accessed October 31, 2018, http://www.pewforum.org/religious-landscape-study/attendance-at-religious-services/.

7. *Merriam-Webster*, s.v. "pluralism," accessed October 31, 2018, https://www.merriam-webster.com/dictionary/pluralism.

8. Alistair E. McGrath, "Pluralism and the Decade of Evangelism," *Anvil* 9, no. 2 (1992): 101, accessed October 31, 2018, https://biblicalstudies.org.uk/pdf/anvil/09-2_101.pdf.

9. Ibid.

10. "Visions of Jesus Stir Muslim Hearts," CBN, accessed November 2, 2018, http://www1.cbn.com/onlinediscipleship/visions-of-jesus-stir-muslim-hearts.

11. McGrath, "Pluralism," 114.

12. Suicide rates increased by 25 percent across the United States over nearly two decades ending in 2016, according to research published June 7, 2018, by the United States Centers for Disease Control and Prevention. Susan Scutti, "US Suicide Rates Increased More Than 25% Since 1999, CDC Says," CNN.com, updated June 22, 2018, https://www.cnn.com/2018/06/07/health/suicide-report-cdc/index.html.

13. Erik Vance, "Why Are Suicide Rates Rising?" LiveScience.com, June 9, 2018, https://www.livescience.com/62781-why-are-suicide-rates-rising.html.

Chapter 3

1. This focus on "the way to heaven" occurs in Wesley's often-quoted "man of one book" paragraph in *Sermons I*, vol. 1 of *The Bicentennial Edition of the Works of John Wesley*, ed. Albert C. Outler (Nashville: Abingdon Press, 1984), 104-6.

2. Michael J. Gorman, *Becoming the Gospel: Paul, Participation, and Mission* (Grand Rapids: Eerdmans, 2015), 298.

3. See Andy Johnson's important *Holiness and the Missio Dei* (Eugene, OR: Cascade, 2016) as well as Gorman's *Becoming the Gospel* and *Abide and Go: Missional Theosis in the Gospel of John*, The Didsbury Lectures 2016 (Eugene, OR: Cascade, 2018).

4. This refers to the canonical collection, not necessarily authorship.

5. It is important not to confuse modern biographies with the ancient genre bios of which our gospels are an example. See Richard A. Burridge, *What Are the Gospels? A Comparison with Graeco-Roman Biography*, 2nd ed. (Grand Rapids: Eerdmans, 2004).

6. The memorable title that N. T. Wright gives to his book, *The Day the Revolution Began: Rethinking the Meaning of Jesus' Death* (London: SPCK, 2017), captures the central point of Christian Scripture.

7. For an excellent recent discussion of the connection between the Old Testament and the New Testament, see Richard B. Hays, *Reading Backwards: Figural Christology and the Fourfold Gospel Witness* (Waco, TX: Baylor University Press, 2014).

8. Scholars have long noted Isaiah's importance in shaping the New Testament writers' reflections on Jesus and his mission to the point that it has been called "the fifth gospel." See John F. A. Sawyer, *The Fifth Gospel: Isaiah in the History of Christianity* (Cambridge, UK: Cambridge University Press, 1996).

9. A notable citation in the Gospels is from Isaiah 61:1-2 (to be discussed below).

10. See Craig A. Evans, "Mark's Incipit and the Priene Calendar Inscription: From Jewish Gospel to Greco-Roman Gospel," *Journal of Greco-Roman and Christianity and Judaism* 1 (2000): 67-81.

11. The whole story has to be read through our "Jesus glasses," a term I first heard from one of my students. This is the lens of God's ultimate action in Christ. It's how Jesus reads his Bible and how Paul is able to make sense of his whole ancestral story.

12. Johnson, *Holiness and the Missio Dei*, 4.

13. The repeated refrain of the covenant with all flesh confirms the implied covenant in the creation stories (see Gen 8:21; 9:9-10).

14. Disobedience leads to suffering, but so does active participation in the mission of God. While exile is a consequence of idolatry and covenant unfaithfulness, images of the righteous sufferer are clear in the Psalms, coming to their

fullest expression in Isaiah's Suffering Servant and the suffering and vindicated figure in Daniel 7. The same tension is present in 1 Peter 3:9-22.

15. Moses names his firstborn to show that he self-identified as an alien residing in a foreign land (Midian) and a fugitive in Egypt (Exod. 2:22).

16. Johnson, *Holiness and the Missio Dei*, 20.

17. "For the Lord your God . . . executes justice for the orphan and the widow, and . . . loves the strangers, providing them food and clothing. You shall also love the stranger, for you were strangers in the land of Egypt" (Deut. 10:17-19, NRSV).

18. Johnson, *Holiness and the Missio Dei*, 38. The nations will honor God, "when through you I display my holiness before their eyes" (Ezek. 36:23, NRSV); when they fail, the name is profaned. The whole direction and purpose of the law is exclusive devotion to God: "Hear, O Israel: The LORD is our God, the LORD alone. You shall love the LORD your God with all your heart, and with all your soul, and with all your might" (Deut. 6:4-5, NRSV), and "you shall love your neighbor as yourself: I am the LORD" (Lev. 19:18, NRSV). According to Jesus, "on these two commandments hang all the law and the prophets" (Matt. 22:40, NRSV).

19. After the death of Solomon, in 922 BC his kingdom is divided into two kingdoms, Israel in the north and Judah in the south. Samaria is the capital of Israel; Jerusalem the capital of Judah.

20. Even in exile, Jeremiah reminds them that their mission continues: "Seek the welfare of the city where I have sent you into exile, and pray to the LORD on its behalf, for in its welfare you will find your welfare" (see Jer. 29:5-7, NRSV).

21. The claim is controversial, but N. T. Wright has made a very strong case for this perception. See now James M. Scott, ed., *Exile: A Conversation with N. T. Wright* (Downers Grove, IL: InterVarsity Press, 2017).

22. Matthew cites Hosea 11:1, a passage referring explicitly to Israel, "Out of Egypt I have called my son" (Matt. 2:15, NRSV), and applies it to Jesus. Jesus is the Messiah, the Son of David, explicitly identified with Israel.

23. The identity of the author of this gospel is contested.

24. Jesus is the "Lamb of God" (John 1:29, 36, NRSV), "Son of God" (1:34, 49, NRSV), "the Messiah" (v. 41, NRSV), "King of Israel" (v. 49, NRSV). Significantly, he is the one "about whom Moses in the law and also the prophets wrote" (v. 45, NRSV). For Luke, this full biblical explanation awaits Jesus's post-resurrection teaching on the road to Emmaus: "Then beginning with Moses

and all the prophets, [Jesus] interpreted to them the things about himself in all the scriptures" (Luke 24:27, NRSV). But John makes the connection early and explicit.

25. Although the three Gospel temptation narratives differ in detail, all challenge Jesus's identity and mission.

26. See Kent E. Brower, *Mark: A Commentary in the Wesleyan Tradition*, New Beacon Bible Commentary (Kansas City: Beacon Hill Press of Kansas City, 2012), 65-66.

27. When his family grows concerned, Jesus pointedly responds, "Who are my mother and my brothers? . . . Whoever does the will of God is my brother and sister and mother" (Mark 3:33-35, NRSV).

28. What better time to start a revolt for freedom than Passover, the festival celebrating Israel's liberation from slavery? It was the beginning of the revolution (see endnote 6 above), but not as they expected. John's Jesus explicitly states that "my kingdom is not from this world" (John 18:36, NRSV).

29. Perhaps the longer ending of Mark (16:9-20)—a second-century pastiche—gives a clue to what this leadership looks like: Jesus continues to be present with them in the mission of God. This possibility was suggested by Professor Markus Bockmuehl in Lecture One of his 2018 Didsbury Lectures, "The Presence and Absence of Jesus in the Four Evangelists" (October 29, 2018) at Nazarene Theological College, Manchester, England.

30. See Bockmuehl in Lecture Two.

31. Jesus, the one filled with the Spirit, has just shown what spirit-power is *not* in the temptation narratives. It is empowerment for fulfillment of the mission of God, not about self.

32. Perhaps that is why there is no evidence that an actual year of Jubilee ever occurred in Israel's history, despite the extensive Torah regulations for it (see Lev. 25; 27).

33. The Baptist promised judgment (Luke 3:9, 17), but Jesus does not deliver. When John later sends messengers to Jesus to ask if Jesus is indeed the coming one, Jesus's response is to report to John what is happening (7:18-23), in line with the sermon at Nazareth and the prophetic hopes of Isaiah (see Isa. 35:5-10).

34. Kent Brower, *Holiness in the Gospels* (Kansas City: Beacon Hill Press of Kansas City, 2005), 53. "Jesus is announcing a mission to the impure and hated Gentiles as well. . . . So they reject Jesus, His mission, and His message. They would rather continue to be God's holy people their own way—keeping pure from

contamination, defending God's holiness against the foreigners, the tax collectors, prostitutes, and sinners, keeping their theological categories clear" (ibid.).

35. Ibid., 55. "For Jesus, the problem is that his opponents seem to miss the central point about God's holiness. God is not a finger-wagging, fussy, and stern patriarch who watches vigilantly lest someone break a rule. Rather, His holiness is His essential character, shown as a gracious and loving God, slow to anger and plenteous in mercy" (ibid.).

36. See the fuller discussion of these parables in ibid., 55-59.

37. Ibid., 56.

38. Ibid., 57.

39. Ibid.

40. See MiJa Wi, *The Path to Salvation in Luke's Gospel: What Must We Do?* Library of New Testament Studies 621 (London: T and T Clark/Bloomsbury, 2019).

41. This is borrowed from the title of Gorman's *Abide and Go* (2018).

42. Kallistos Ware, *The Orthodox Way* (Crestwood, NY: St Vladimir's Seminary Press, 1979), 27.

43. Gorman, *Abide and Go*, 131.

44. Jesus's prayer is that his followers "may all be one. As you, Father, are in me and I am in you, may they also be in us, so that the world may believe that you have sent me. The glory that you have given me I have given them, so that they may be one, as we are one, I in them and you in me, that they may become completely one, so that the world may know that you have sent me and have loved them even as you have loved me" (John 17:21-23, NRSV).

45. See Brower, *Holiness in the Gospels*, 65-69.

46. Ibid., 76.

47. Ibid.

48. Gorman, *Abide and Go*, 144. He continues, John 20:23 "should not be interpreted as dispensing to the disciples either ultimate control over, or a carte blanche, for the forgiveness of sins. . . . God, not the community of disciples, is the one who has been offended and from whom forgiveness is needed" (ibid.).

49. See ibid., 131-32: "Like Jesus, disciples are in a relationship of mutual indwelling. Jesus . . . continues his work in and through his disciples. . . . The disciples need to depend on [God] by constantly abiding and praying. . . . And all of this is dependent on the presence and power of the resurrected Christ present by the Paraclete."

50. This section is more developed in Kent Brower, *Living as God's Holy People: Holiness and Community in Paul*, The Didsbury Lectures 2008 (London: Paternoster, 2010).

51. Ibid., 87.

52. Gorman, *Becoming the Gospel*, and Johnson, *Holiness and the Missio Dei*, both call this Paul's master story.

53. Johnson, *Holiness and the Missio Dei*, 128-29, writes, "In a downward *divine* movement" paralleled by a "corresponding downward *human* movement" the Messiah reveals "the essence of God's own character . . . through his vulnerable love. . . . The inseparability of this faithful obedience and self-giving love is evident throughout Paul's letters."

54. See Svetlana Khobnya, *The Father Who Redeems and the Son Who Obeys* (Eugene, OR: Pickwick, 2013). See also the monumental treatment in N. T. Wright, *Paul and the Faithfulness of God* (London: SPCK, 2013). Paul writes, "By sending his own Son in the likeness of sinful flesh, . . . [God] condemned sin in the flesh, so that the just requirement of the law might be fulfilled in us, who walk not according to the flesh but according to the Spirit" (Rom 8:3-4, NRSV).

55. Gorman, *Becoming the Gospel*, 2.

56. Ibid., 31, states that this is a "a deep participation in Christ, especially in his death, that is shared with other believers and that comes to fruition in concrete practices of sacrificial, generous, self-giving love and even suffering."

57. Brower, *Living as God's Holy People*, 89.

58. See Moyer V. Hubbard, *New Creation in Paul's Letters and Thought*, Society for New Testament Studies Monograph Series 119 (Cambridge, UK: Cambridge University Press, 2002), 238.

59. Ibid., 235.

60. See Brower, *Living as God's Holy People*, 94: "We live as resurrection people now: people of life, not death; of hope, not despair; of holiness, not defilement; in anticipation of the redemption of our bodies and the restoration of all things. This, too, fits into the purposes of God who calls his holy people to share in the ministry of reconciliation even as we await the glorious future when Christ shall be all and in all."

61. Ibid., 87. There is no place in Christ for racism, sexism or any other division that manifests the old way of living in Adam.

62. Ibid. Gentiles "have been brought near by the blood of Christ. For he is our peace; in his flesh he has made both groups into one and has broken down the dividing wall . . . that he might create in himself one new humanity in place of

the two, thus making peace, and might reconcile both groups to God in one body through the cross, thus putting to death that hostility through it" (Eph. 2:13-16, NRSV).

63. Brower, *Living as God's Holy People*, 96: "Christians, then and now, can never give ultimate allegiance to any state or system—nationalism and patriotism all too often drift into elitism, racism and even idolatry. Ultimate loyalty of believers can only ever be offered to Christ, who is Lord, not Caesar" (ibid.).

64. Thus, in 2 Corinthians 5:17-19, Paul notes that God's holy people, his new creation, are not simply reconciled to God; they are to be agents of that reconciliation in the world. They are to minister the peace of Christ and to model the love of Christ among their fellow human beings in the real world. Paul writes, "We are children of God, and if children, then heirs, heirs of God and joint heirs with Christ—if, in fact, we suffer with him so that we may also be glorified with him" (Rom. 8:16-17, NRSV).

65. The free gift is greater than the trespass (Rom. 5:15-19), undoing the disastrous disobedience of Adam and Israel.

66. Brower, *Living as God's Holy People*, 92.

67. Ibid., 94.

68. The authorship of the book of Revelation is a matter of scholarly dispute. "John" here is "the author," but unlikely to be the same as the author of the Gospel of John.

69. Dean Flemming, "On Earth as It Is in Heaven: Holiness and the People of God in Revelation," in *Holiness and Ecclesiology in the New Testament*, ed. Kent Brower and Andy Johnson (Grand Rapids: Eerdmans, 2007), 343-62.

70. The attractiveness and power of the empire are seductive and overwhelming. John's warning to his readers has an uncanny contemporary ring. Flemming writes, "Wherever governments or global conglomerates fill their own coffers at the expense of powerless people; wherever political or commercial empires behave in ways that demand idolatrous allegiance; wherever nations use military, economic, or political coercion as a tool of self-serving policies; wherever societies or individuals embrace an ethos of greedy consumption—there is Babylon reborn" (ibid., 360).

71. Ibid., 354.

72. Ibid., 353.

73. Ibid., 355.

74. Ibid.

Chapter 4

1. See Exodus 5:19-21, for example.

2. Genesis 1 does this by calling the sun and moon "lights" and affirming that they were created by God, rather than calling them by names that denoted them as gods. See also Deut. 4:35, 39; 2 Kings 19:15; Psalms 86:10; Isaiah 44:6; 45:14.

3. Psalms 95–100 all echo this universal note.

4. See, for instance, Jonah 4:11. In addition to Jonah, the book of Isaiah reveals God's interest in other nations. See, for instance, Isaiah 12:4; 42:6; 45:22; 49:6; 51:4-5; 56:6-7.

5. Three times in Colossians 1:28 Paul says the gospel is being proclaimed to everyone, to all human beings ("all" or "every" [Gk., *panta*]; "human" [Gk., *anthrōpon*]).

6. See, for example, Augustine's *Enchiridion*, chaps. 95–99, 100, 103, trans. J. F. Shaw, Logos Library, http://www.logoslibrary.org/augustine/enchiridion/.

7. Augustine, *On the Predestination of the Saints*, bk. 1, chap. 16. *New Advent*. http://www.newadvent.org/fathers/15121.htm.

Martin Luther (1483–1546) admitted that human reason cannot explain "the mercy and equity of God in damning the undeserving, that is, ungodly persons, who being born in ungodliness, can by no means avoid being ungodly, and staying so, and being damned, but are compelled by natural necessity to sin and perish." Rather than questioning God, he must be "reverenced and held in awe, as being most merciful to those whom He justified and saves in their own utter unworthiness; and we must show some measure of deference to His Divine wisdom by believing Him just when to us He seems unjust." Martin Luther, *The Bondage of the Will*, in *Martin Luther: Selections from His Writings*, ed. John Dillenberger (Garden City, NY: Anchor Books, 1961), 200.

8. John Calvin, *Institutes of the Christian Religion*, bk. 3, chap. 21, sec. 7, Christian Classics Ethereal Library, https://www.ccel.org/ccel/calvin/institutes.

9. Ibid.

10. These doctrinal points are recorded in the Canons of Dort, and in chapter 3 of the Westminster Confession.

11. See, for instance, the teaching of Gregory Nazianzus (ca. AD 329-90) as presented in Christopher T. Bounds, "The Scope of the Atonement in the Early Church Fathers," *Wesleyan Theological Journal* 47, no. 2 (Fall 2012): 12, or the teaching of Irenaeus (ca. AD 130–ca. AD 202) in Bounds, "Scope of the Atonement," 9.

12. Irenaeus, *Against Heresies*, bk. 5, chap. 12, sec. 3, http://www.earlychristianwritings.com/text/irenaeus-book5.html.

13. Bounds, "Scope of the Atonement," 12.

14. Quoted in ibid., 13.

15. Ibid., 13-14.

16. Ibid., 14.

17. Ibid., 16. Gnosticism was a complex religion with views of creation, sin, and salvation that were foreign to the gospel. Some Gnostics attempted to rewrite Christ as a Gnostic savior and thus brought great confusion to people.

18. John Wesley, "Free Grace," Sermon 128, sec. 26, in *The Sermons of John Wesley*, ed. Thomas Jackson (1872; Wesley Center Online, 1999), http://wesley.nnu.edu/john-wesley/the-sermons-of-john-wesley-1872-edition/sermon-128-free-grace/.

19. James E. Pedlar, "Predestination and God's Sovereignty," Seedbed, May 21, 2013. https://www.seedbed.com/predestination-and-gods-sovereignty/. "Generally speaking, the Calvinist tradition has seen sovereignty through the model of a ruling monarch, whereas Wesley conceived of sovereignty primarily through the model of a loving parent." See also hymn 129, in *A Collection of Hymns for the Use of the People Called Methodists*, ed. John Wesley (1779; repr., London: Wesleyan Conference Office, 1876): "Thee, the paternal grace divine / A universal blessing gave, / A light in every heart to shine, / A Saviour every soul to save." Google Books, https://www.google.com/books/edition/A_collection_of_hymns_for_the_use_of_the/p69bAAAAQAAJ?hl=en&gbpv=1&dq=A+Collection+of+Hymns+for+Use+of+the+People+Called+Methodists,+edited+by+John+Wesley&printsec=frontcover#spf=1588104982264.

20. Wesley, "Free Grace," sec. 18.

21. See John Wesley, "The Scripture Way of Salvation," Sermon 43, pt. 3, sec. 2, In *The Sermons of John Wesley*, http://wesley.nnu.edu/john-wesley/the-sermons-of-john-wesley-1872-edition/sermon-43-the-scripture-way-of-salvation/.

22. John Wesley, "The General Spread of the Gospel," Sermon 63, sec. 11, in vol. 6 of *The Works of John Wesley*, ed. Thomas Jackson, 3rd ed. (1872; repr., Peabody, MA: Hendrickson, 1984), 280.

23. Wesley, "Free Grace."

24. Wesley, "On Predestination," Sermon 58, sec. 14, in vol. 6 of *Works of John Wesley*, 229-30.

25. Ibid.

26. See Wesley, "General Spread of the Gospel," secs. 10-12.

27. "Prevenient Grace," Article VII, Articles of Faith, in *Manual/2017–2021: Church of the Nazarene* (Kansas City: Nazarene Publishing House, 2017), para. 7.

28. This is observed within the Reformed camp and outside it. Reformed corporate election proponents include Karl Barth, Lesslie Newbigin, Tom (N. T.) Wright, and Suzanne McDonald. Examples from the Arminian side include Clark Pinnock, A. Chadwick Thornhill, and Ben Witherington. Coming from a variety of theological backgrounds, advocates of corporate election differ among themselves. For an excellent introduction to the concept of corporate election, see Brian Abasciano, "Clearing up Misconceptions about Corporate Election," *Asbury Theological Journal*, no. 41 (2009): 59-90.

29. Neo-Orthodox theologian Karl Barth pioneered this shift in his *Christian Dogmatics* II.2, *The Doctrine of God.*

30. See Gal. 3–4; Eph. 2.

31. Karl Barth saw believers and unbelievers as somehow included in Christ, which resulted in his doctrine of election seeming to lean toward universalism—the idea that even those who remain in unbelief will ultimately be saved. Barth's theological intention here, however, is widely debated.

32. Wynkoop, Mildred Bangs, *Foundations of Wesleyan-Arminian Theology* (Kansas City: Beacon Hill Press of Kansas City, 1967), 53.

33. Nazarene theologian H. Orton Wiley referred to this as "class predestination." H. Orton Wiley, et al., "The Debate Over Divine Election," *Christianity Today*, October 12, 1959, 3.

34. For an extended discussion of this history of election, see A. Chadwick Thornhill, *The Chosen People: Election, Paul and Second Temple Judaism* (Downers Grove, IL: InterVarsity Press, 2015).

35. McDonald's ideas can be found in *Re-Imaging Election: Divine Election as Representing God to Others and Others to God* (Grand Rapids: Eerdmans, 2010).

36. For an in-depth discussion of these ideas, see N. T. Wright, *The Day the Revolution Began: Reconsidering the Meaning of Jesus's Crucifixion* (New York: HarperOne, 2016).

37. Roger E. Olson, "A Classic Book about 'Corporate Election' Revised, Enlarged, and Re-Published," Patheos.com, February 5, 2016, http://www.patheos.com/blogs/rogereolson/2016/02/a-classic-book-about-corporate-election-revised-enlarged-and-re-published/. Olson is reviewing William Klein, *The New Chosen People: A Corporate View of Election*, rev. ed. (Eugene, OR: Wipf and Stock, 2015). Klein is professor of New Testament, Denver Seminary.

38. Trevin Wax, "Interview with N. T. Wright—Responding to Piper on Justification," *The Gospel Coalition* (blog), January 13, 2009, https://www.thegospelcoalition.org/blogs/trevin-wax/interview-with-nt-wright-responding-to-piper-on-justification. Wright expands on this, among other places, in his book *The Day the Revolution Began.*

39. Jack W. Cottrell, "Conditional Election," in *Grace Unlimited*, ed. Clark H. Pinnock (Eugene, OR: Wipf and Stock, 1999), 54.

40. David J. Bosch, *Transforming Mission: Paradigm Shifts in Theology of Mission* (Maryknoll, NY: Orbis Books, 1991).

41. Lesslie Newbigin, "The Logic of Election," in *The Gospel in a Pluralist Society* (Grand Rapids: Eerdmans, 1989), 86.

Chapter 5

1. The word "you" is in the plural throughout this section in Ephesians. One could translate this in the Southern dialect of "you all" as a way of emphasizing the corporate nature of the condition of sin we all share in prior to redemption.

2. Wesley was not unique in his use of prevenient grace. But he did add his own distinction in the "order of salvation." In Catholic theology "actual grace" is divided into two parts or pairs: "operating prevenient grace" and "cooperating subsequent grace."

3. Like Wesley, Anglican theologian Fleming Rutledge recognizes the importance of prevenient grace. "We need to recover that word 'prevenient' because no other word or phrase captures so well the essential fact about grace: it prevenes (goes before), or precedes, recognition of sin, precedes confession of sin, precedes repentance for sin, and precedes forsaking of sin." *The Crucifixion: Understanding the Death of Jesus* (2015; repr., Grand Rapids: Eerdmans, 2017), 168. All persons, Rutledge says, are "held by God's gracious intention toward them, whether they know themselves as sinners or not" (ibid.). "God is moving upon a person's heart before the person even realizes what is happening" (ibid., 174).

4. Albert Outler, ed., *John Wesley*, The Library of Protestant Thought (New York: Oxford University Press, 1964), viii.

5. Lovett H. Weems Jr., *John Wesley's Message Today* (Nashville: Abingdon Press, 1991), 23.

6. Paul M. Bassett, "Re-Wesleyanizing Nazarene Higher Education" (paper presented at the Nazarene Faith, Learning, and Living Conference, San Diego, CA, 1985). Bassett's phrase "morally neutral context" was originally intended for

those in a teaching context. But the inference for the broader result of prevenient grace remains.

7. Ibid.

8. Tom Noble suggests the tendency of treating grace as an objective force or substance (like a Christian motor oil to help your discipleship run more smoothly) came from Medieval Augustinianism. Different types of grace emerged that could be infused into Christians. The tendency expanded in seventeenth-century Protestant scholasticism. "That scholastic model of grace brings its own problems, particularly a tendency to depersonalize the action of God, replacing the personal action of the Spirit with this impersonal substance called 'grace.'" T. A. Noble, *Holy Trinity: Holy People: The Theology of Christian Perfecting* (Eugene, OR: Cascade Books, 2013), 100.

9. Jack Jackson, *Offering Christ: John Wesley's Evangelistic Vision* (Nashville: Kingswood Books, 2017), 53.

10. John Wesley, "Free Grace," Sermon 110, para. 1, in *Sermons III*, ed. Albert C. Outler, vol. 3 of *The Bicentennial Edition of the Works of John Wesley* (Nashville: Abingdon Press, 1986), 544.

11. Jackson, *Offering Christ*, 53.

12. Mildred Bangs Wynkoop, *Foundations of Wesleyan-Arminian Theology* (Kansas City: Beacon Hill Press of Kansas City, 1967), 69.

13. Using the language of "free will" denies that we are "dead in our trespasses and sins" and implies that we can move toward Christ in our own strength. Were that to be true, we would be "contributing" to our salvation. In fact, we are reconciled to God by grace through faith alone. Faith itself is God's gift.

14. Ibid.

15. Karl Barth, *Church Dogmatic: The Doctrine of God*, II.2 (1957; T and T Clark International, 2004), 187.

16. Ibid., 188.

17. Ibid., 186.

18. John Wesley, "Free Grace," Sermon 128, sec. 2, in *The Sermons of John Wesley*, ed. Thomas Jackson (1872; Wesley Center Online, 1999), http://wesley.nnu.edu/john-wesley/the-sermons-of-john-wesley-1872-edition/sermon-128-free-grace/.

19. N. T. Wright, *Paul: A Biography* (San Francisco: HarperOne, 2018), 96.

20. John Wesley, *The Works of the Rev. John Wesley* (Kansas City: Nazarene Publishing House, n.d.; and Grand Rapids: Zondervan, 1958, concurrent editions), 6:513.

21. The word "providence" comes from two Latin words: *pro*, which means "forward" or "on behalf of," and *vide*, which means "to see." Providence is sometimes distinguished into two categories of "general providence," or God's care for the universe, and "special providence," or God's intervention in the life of people.

22. Wesley, *Works of the Rev. John Wesley*, 6:512.

23. The part of Mendoza is played by Robert De Niro.

Chapter 6

1. New Testament scholar N. T. Wright explains that our faith is faith in the faithful, obedient Messiah, who was faithful to God's plan to rescue the world from sin and death, faithfulness that entailed the Messiah's sacrificial death on the cross. "All those who believe the gospel message of [Jesus's] death and resurrection are now themselves accorded the status of *dikaios*: righteous, forgiven, within the covenant" of God's faithfulness "fully and finally unveiled in the cross." N. T. Wright, *Paul: In Fresh Perspective* (Minneapolis: Fortress Press, 2009), 120.

2. In the Missional Church Survey, hospitality ranked fifth out of seventeen spiritual gifts surveyed, with 38.8 percent of respondents indicating that they had the gift of hospitality. Evangelism, by comparison, was a spiritual gift only 8.8 percent of respondents claimed to have!

3. For more, see Randy Maddox, *Responsible Grace: John Wesley's Practical Theology* (Nashville: Kingswood Books, 1994), 65-66.

4. Martin Luther, "Two Kinds of Righteousness," in *Martin Luther's Basic Theological Writings*, ed. Timothy F. Lull (Minneapolis: Fortress Press, 1989), 156.

5. Ibid.

6. Martin Luther, "Bondage of the Will," *Martin Luther: Selections from His Writings*, ed. John Dillenberger (Garden City, NY: Anchor Books, 1961), 179.

7. John Calvin, "Justification by Faith," in *John Calvin: Selections from His Writings*, ed. John Dillenberger, American Academy of Religion Aids for the Study of Religion 2 (Missoula, MT: Scholars Press for the American Academy of Religion, 1975), 436.

8. Calvin, *John Calvin*, 424-25.

9. John Wesley, "Remarks on Dr. Erskine's Defence of the Preface to the Edinburgh Edition of Aspasio Vindicated," May 1766, in vol. 8 of *The Works of the Rev. John Wesley in Ten Volumes* (New York: J. and J. Harper, 1827), 545,

Internet Archive, https://archive.org/details/worksofrevjohnwe08wesl/page/n3/mode/2up?q=I+believe+justification+by+faith+alone.

10. John Wesley, "Justification by Faith," in *John Wesley's Sermons: An Anthology*, ed. Albert C. Outler and Richard P. Heitzenrater (Nashville: Abingdon Press, 1991), 115. Wesley's knowledge of Latin may have shaped his understanding of the word. From the Latin words *per* (completely) and *donare* (to give), the word can carry a connotation of "giving completely," placing the emphasis on a hospitable act of giving, rather than only a legal act of overlooking.

11. Ibid., 119.

12. The most complete account of an East-West synthesis in Wesley's theology is still Randy Maddox, *Responsible Grace: John Wesley's Practical Theology*.

13. Notice the common root of the words "hospital" and "hospitality." "Hospitality" as I am using it is more than offering food and rest. It carries the connotation of healing as well.

14. Mildred Bangs Wynkoop, *A Theology of Love: The Dynamic of Wesleyanism*, 2nd ed. (Kansas City: Beacon Hill Press of Kansas City, 2015), 313.

15. John Wesley, "Principles of a Methodist Farther Explained," in *The Works of John Wesley*, ed. Thomas Jackson, 3rd ed. (1872; repr., Peabody, MA: Hendrickson, 1984), 8:472.

16. Jack Jackson, *Offering Christ: John Wesley's Evangelistic Vision* (Nashville: Kingswood Books, 2017), 31.

17. Ibid., 42 (emphasis added).

18. Maddox, *Responsible Grace*, 220.

Chapter 7

1. John Wesley, "The General Spread of the Gospel," Sermon 63, sec. 27, in *The Sermons of John Wesley*, ed. Thomas Jackson (1872; Wesley Center Online, 1999), http://wesley.nnu.edu/john-wesley/the-sermons-of-john-wesley-1872-edition/sermon-63-the-general-spread-of-the-gospel/.

2. John Wesley, "Free Grace," Sermon 128, sec. 2, in *The Sermons of John Wesley*, http://wesley.nnu.edu/john-wesley/the-sermons-of-john-wesley-1872-edition/sermon-128-free-grace/.

3. Jerome H. Neyrey, "What's Wrong with This Picture? John 4, Cultural Stereotypes of Women, and Public and Private Space," University of Notre Dame, https://www3.nd.edu/~jneyrey1/picture.html.

4. Sang-Ehil Han, Paul Louis Metzger, and Terry C. Muck, "Christian Hospitality and Pastoral Practices from an Evangelical Perspective," *Theological Education* 47, no. 1 (January 1, 2012).

5. Archie Smith Jr., "Hospitality: A Spiritual Resource for Building Community," *Journal of the Interdenominational Theological Center* 25, no. 3 (Spring 1998): 139–51.

6. Ibid.

7. Ibid.

8. Nabeel Qureshi, *Seeking Allah, Finding Jesus: A Devout Muslim Encounters Christianity* (Grand Rapids: Zondervan, 2016).

9. In the first century "Ethiopian" meant "Nubian." Nubians were dark-skinned people.

10. Ajith Fernando, *Acts*, The NIV Application Commentary (Grand Rapids: Zondervan, 1998).

Chapter 8

1. See the introduction to Bryan Stone's *Evangelism after Christendom* in which he suggests "The E-word has become a dirty word" in an increasingly pluralistic and post-Christendom context. Bryan Stone, *Evangelism after Christendom: The Theology and Practice of Christian Witness* (Grand Rapids: Brazos Press, 2007), 10.

2. Alasdair MacIntyre, *After Virtue: A Study in Moral Theory*, 3rd ed. (Notre Dame, IN: University of Notre Dame Press, 2007), 187.

3. Brad J. Kallenberg, "The Master Argument of MacIntyre's *After Virtue*," in *Virtues and Practices in the Christian Tradition: Christian Ethics after MacIntyre*, ed. Nancey Murphy, Brad J. Kallenberg, and Mark Thiessen Nation (1997; repr., Notre Dame, IN: University of Notre Dame Press, 2003) 21.

4. John Wesley, "Causes of the Inefficacy of Christianity," Sermon 122, in *Sermons IV*, ed. Albert C. Outler, vol. 4 of *The Bicentennial Edition of the Works of John Wesley* (Nashville: Abingdon Press, 1987), 86.

5. John Wesley, "The Means of Grace," Sermon 16, in *Sermons I*, ed. Albert C. Outler, vol. 1 of *The Bicentennial Edition of the Works of John Wesley* (Nashville: Abingdon Press, 1984), 381.

6. John Wesley, "On Zeal," Sermon 92, in *Sermon III*, ed. Albert C. Outler, vol. 3 of *The Bicentennial Edition of the Works of John Wesley* (Nashville: Abingdon Press, 1986), 314.

7. Find the full development of Stark's argument in Rodney Stark, *The Rise of Christianity: A Sociologist Reconsiders History* (Princeton, NJ: Princeton University Press, 1996).

8. John Wesley, "On Visiting the Sick," Sermon 98, in *Sermons III*, ed. Albert C. Outler, vol. 3 of *The Bicentennial Edition of the Works of John Wesley* (Nashville: Abingdon Press, 1986), 387.

Chapter 9

1. My description of encounter evangelism is informed by Richard V. Peace, *Conversion in the New Testament: Paul and the Twelve* (Grand Rapids: Eerdmans, 1999), 285-308.

2. For baptismal ritual, see Jesse C. Middendorf, *The Church Rituals Handbook*, 2nd ed. (Kansas City: Beacon Hill Press of Kansas City, 2009), 17-18.

3. Howard A. Snyder, *Yes in Christ: Wesleyan Reflections on Gospel, Mission, and Culture* (Toronto: Clements Publishing Group, 2011), 27.

4. Ibid.

5. John Wesley's charge to his preachers quoted in Robert E. Coleman, *"Nothing to Do But to Save Souls": John Wesley's Charge to His Preachers* (Grand Rapids: Francis Asbury Press, 2006), 16.

6. William J. Abraham, "The Epistemology of Conversion: Is There Something New?" in *Conversion in the Wesleyan Tradition*, ed. Kenneth J. Collins and John H. Tyson (Nashville: Abingdon Press, 2001), 184.

7. Ibid., 184 (emphasis added).

8. Gordon T. Smith, *Transforming Conversion: Rethinking the Language and Contours of Christian Initiation* (Grand Rapids: Baker Academic, 2010), 2.

9. Ibid., 12.

10. Ibid., 13.

11. Ron Benefiel, "John Wesley's Mission of Evangelism" (unpublished manuscript, December 2007), 3.

12. Ibid., 10.

13. Ibid., 13.

14. Ibid., 15.

15. Scott J. Jones, *The Evangelistic Love of God and Neighbor: A Theology of Witness and Discipleship* (Nashville: Abingdon Press, 2003), 18.

16. Ibid., 139-40.

17. For a full description of practices of evangelism that are personal, see Grant Zweigle, *Worship, Wonder, and Way: Reimagining Evangelism as Missional Practice* (Kansas City: Beacon Hill Press of Kansas City, 2015).

18. John Dickson, *The Best Kept Secret of Christian Mission: Promoting the Gospel with More Than Our Lips* (Grand Rapids: Zondervan, 2010), 75.

19. Ibid.

20. See John Wesley, "The Principles of a Methodist Farther Explained," in *The Methodist Societies—History, Nature, and Design*, ed. Rupert E. Davies, vol. 9 of *The Bicentennial Edition of the Works of John Wesley* (Nashville: Abingdon Press, 1989), 227.

21. See Gregory S. Clapper, *The Renewal of the Heart Is the Mission of the Church: Wesley's Heart Religion in the Twenty-First Century* (Eugene, OR: Wipf and Stock, 2010).

22. Gregory S. Clapper, *As If the Heart Mattered: A Wesleyan Spirituality* (Eugene, OR: Wipf and Stock, 2014).

23. Bryan P. Stone, *Evangelism after Christendom: The Theology and Practice of Christian Witness* (Grand Rapids: Brazos Press, 2007), 12.

Chapter 10

1. John Wesley, "The Means of Grace," Sermon 16, in vol. 5 of *The Works of John Wesley*, ed. Thomas Jackson, 3rd ed. (1872; repr., Peabody, MA: Hendrickson, 1984), 185.

2. Ibid., 187.

3. Ibid., 196.

4. Ontology is the study of the nature of existence, or being as such. It is a study of or theory about "the really real" or "most real."

5. James K. A. Smith, *Desiring the Kingdom: Worship, Worldview, and Cultural Formation* (Grand Rapids: Baker Academic, 2009), 193.

6. Ibid., 195.

7. Alasdair MacIntyre, *After Virtue: A Study in Moral Theory*, 3rd ed. (Notre Dame, IN: University of Notre Dame Press, 2007), 216.

8. Brent D. Peterson, *Created to Worship: God's Invitation to Become Fully Human* (Kansas City: Beacon Hill Press of Kansas City, 2012), 176.

9. Wesley, "The Means of Grace," 185.

Chapter 11

1. See "More about Nazarenes," Church of the Nazarene, https://nazarene.org/mission.

www.ingramcontent.com/pod-product-compliance
Lightning Source LLC
Chambersburg PA
CBHW070039100426
42740CB00013B/2728

* 9 7 8 0 8 3 4 1 3 8 2 9 2 *